PLAY ON SHAKESPEARE

Titus Andronicus

PLAY ON SHAKESPEARE

All's Well That Ends Well	Virginia Grise
Antony and Cleopatra	Christopher Chen
As You Like It	David Ivers
The Comedy of Errors	Christina Anderson
Coriolanus	Sean San José
Cymbeline	Andrea Thome
Edward III	Octavio Solis
Hamlet	Lisa Peterson
Henry IV	Yvette Nolan
Henry V	Lloyd Suh
Henry VI	Douglas P. Langworthy
Henry VIII	Caridad Svich
Julius Caesar	Shishir Kurup
King John	Brighde Mullins
King Lear	Marcus Gardley
Love's Labour's Lost	Josh Wilder
Macbeth	Migdalia Cruz
Measure for Measure	Aditi Brennan Kapil
The Merchant of Venice	Elise Thoron
The Merry Wives of Windsor	Dipika Guha
A Midsummer Night's Dream	Jeffrey Whitty
Much Ado About Nothing	Ranjit Bolt
Othello	Mfoniso Udofia
Pericles	Ellen McLaughlin
Richard II	Naomi Iizuka
Richard III	Migdalia Cruz
Romeo and Juliet	Hansol Jung
The Taming of the Shrew	Amy Freed
The Tempest	Kenneth Cavander
Timon of Athens	Kenneth Cavander
Titus Andronicus	Amy Freed
Troilus and Cressida	Lillian Groag
Twelfth Night	Alison Carey
The Two Gentlemen of Verona	Amelia Roper
The Two Noble Kinsmen	Tim Slover
The Winter's Tale	Tracy Young

Titus Andronicus

by
William Shakespeare

Modern verse translation by
Amy Freed

Dramaturgy by
Lezlie C. Cross

Arizona Center
for Medieval and
Renaissance Studies

ACMRS PRESS

Arizona State University
Tempe, Arizona
2022

Publication of Play On Shakespeare is assisted by generous support from the Hitz Foundation. For more information, please visit www.playonshakespeare.org

———

Published by ACMRS Press
Arizona Center for Medieval and Renaissance Studies,
Arizona State University, Tempe, Arizona
www.acmrspress.com

Library of Congress Cataloging-in-Publication Data

Names: Freed, Amy, 1958- author. | Cross, Lezlie C., dramaturge. |
  Shakespeare, William, 1564-1616. Titus Andronicus.
Title: Titus Andronicus / by William Shakespeare ; modern verse translation
  by Amy Freed ; dramaturgy by Lezlie C. Cross.
Description: Tempe, Arizona : ACMRS Press, 2022. | Series: Play on
  Shakespeare | Summary: "One of Shakespeare's goriest plays, Titus
  Andronicus traces the fall of the Andronicus family in ancient Rome. This
  translation is careful and meticulous, making small but mighty changes in
  moments that enhance the drama of each scene giving this extraordinary
  play an even faster track on which to run"-- Provided by publisher.
Identifiers: LCCN 2022006115 (print) | LCCN 2022006116 (ebook) |
  ISBN 9780866987752 (paperback) | ISBN 9780866987769 (ebook)
Subjects: LCSH: Andronicus, Titus (Fictitious character)--Drama. | Rome--
  History--Germanic Invasions, 3rd-6th centuries--Drama. | Goths--Drama.
  | Generals--Drama. | LCGFT: Tragedies (Drama)
Classification: LCC PR2878.T55 F74 2022 (print) | LCC PR2878.T55 (ebook)
  | DDC 812/.54--dc23/eng/20220210
LC record available at https://lccn.loc.gov/2022006115
LC ebook record available at https://lccn.loc.gov/2022006116

Printed in the United States of America

We wish to acknowledge our gratitude
for the extraordinary generosity of the
Hitz Foundation

~

Special thanks to the Play on Shakespeare staff
Lue Douthit, CEO and Creative Director
Kamilah Long, Executive Director
Taylor Bailey, Associate Creative Director and Senior Producer
Summer Martin, Director of Operations
Amrita Ramanan as Senior Cultural Strategist and Dramaturg
Katie Kennedy, Publications Project Manager

~

Originally commissioned by the
Oregon Shakespeare Festival
Bill Rauch, Artistic Director
Cynthia Rider, Executive Director

SERIES PREFACE
PLAY ON SHAKESPEARE

In 2015, the Oregon Shakespeare Festival announced a new com-
missioning program. It was called "Play on!: 36 playwrights trans-
late Shakespeare." It elicited a flurry of reactions. For some people
this went too far: "You can't touch the language!" For others, it
didn't go far enough: "Why not new adaptations?" I figured we
would be on the right path if we hit the sweet spot in the middle.

Some of the reaction was due not only to the scale of the proj-
ect, but its suddenness: 36 playwrights, along with 38 dramaturgs,
had been commissioned and assigned to translate 39 plays, and
they were already hard at work on the assignment. It also came
fully funded by the Hitz Foundation with the shocking sticker
price of $3.7 million.

I think most of the negative reaction, however, had to do with
the use of the word "translate." It's been difficult to define pre-
cisely. It turns out that there is no word for the kind of subtle and
rigorous examination of language that we are asking for. We don't
mean "word for word," which is what most people think of when
they hear the word translate. We don't mean "paraphrase," either.

The project didn't begin with 39 commissions. Linguist John
McWhorter's musings about translating Shakespeare is what
sparked this project. First published in his 1998 book *Word on the
Street* and reprinted in 2010 in *American Theatre* magazine, he
notes that the "irony today is that the Russians, the French, and
other people in foreign countries possess Shakespeare to a much
greater extent than we do, for the simple reason that they get to
enjoy Shakespeare in the language they speak."

This intrigued Dave Hitz, a long-time patron of the Oregon Shakespeare Festival, and he offered to support a project that looked at Shakespeare's plays through the lens of the English we speak today. How much has the English language changed since Shakespeare? Is it possible that there are conventions in the early modern English of Shakespeare that don't translate to us today, especially in the moment of hearing it spoken out loud as one does in the theater?

How might we "carry forward" the successful communication between actor and audience that took place 400 years ago? "Carry forward," by the way, is what we mean by "translate." It is the fourth definition of *translate* in the Oxford English Dictionary.

As director of literary development and dramaturgy at the Oregon Shakespeare Festival, I was given the daunting task of figuring out how to administer the project. I began with Kenneth Cavander, who translates ancient Greek tragedies into English. I figured that someone who does that kind of work would lend an air of seriousness to the project. I asked him how might he go about translating from the source language of early modern English into the target language of contemporary modern English?

He looked at different kinds of speech: rhetorical and poetical, soliloquies and crowd scenes, and the puns in comedies. What emerged from his tinkering became a template for the translation commission. These weren't rules exactly, but instructions that every writer was given.

First, do no harm. There is plenty of the language that doesn't need translating. And there is some that does. Every playwright had different criteria for assessing what to change.

Second, go line-by-line. No editing, no cutting, no "fixing." I want the whole play translated. We often cut the gnarly bits in

Shakespeare for performance. What might we make of those bits if we understood them in the moment of hearing them? Might we be less compelled to cut?

Third, all other variables stay the same: the time period, the story, the characters, their motivations, and their thoughts. We designed the experiment to examine the language.

Fourth, and most important, the language must follow the same kind of rigor and pressure as the original, which means honoring the meter, rhyme, rhetoric, image, metaphor, character, action, and theme. Shakespeare's astonishingly compressed language must be respected. Trickiest of all: making sure to work within the structure of the iambic pentameter.

We also didn't know which of Shakespeare's plays might benefit from this kind of investigation: the early comedies, the late tragedies, the highly poetic plays. So we asked three translators who translate plays from other languages into English to examine a Shakespeare play from each genre outlined in the *First Folio*: Kenneth took on *Timon of Athens,* a tragedy; Douglas Langworthy worked on the *Henry the Sixth* history plays, and Ranjit Bolt tried his hand at the comedy *Much Ado about Nothing.*

Kenneth's *Timon* received a production at the Alabama Shakespeare in 2014 and it was on the plane ride home that I thought about expanding the project to include 39 plays. And I wanted to do them all at once. The idea was to capture a snapshot of contemporary modern English. I couldn't oversee that many commissions, and when Ken Hitz (Dave's brother and president of the Hitz Foundation) suggested that we add a dramaturg to each play, the plan suddenly unfolded in front of me. The next day, I made a simple, but extensive, proposal to Dave on how to commission and develop 39 translations in three years. He responded immediately with "Yes."

My initial thought was to only commission translators who translate plays. But I realized that "carry forward" has other meanings. There was a playwright in the middle of the conversation 400 years ago. What would it mean to carry *that* forward?

For one thing, it would mean that we wanted to examine the texts through the lens of performance. I am interested in learning how a dramatist makes sense of the play. Basically, we asked the writers to create performable companion pieces.

I wanted to tease out what we mean by contemporary modern English, and so we created a matrix of writers who embodied many different lived experiences: age, ethnicity, gender-identity, experience with translations, geography, English as a second language, knowledge of Shakespeare, etc.

What the playwrights had in common was a deep love of language and a curiosity about the assignment. Not everyone was on board with the idea and I was eager to see how the experiment would be for them. They also pledged to finish the commission within three years.

To celebrate the completion of the translations, we produced a festival in June 2019 in partnership with The Classic Stage Company in New York to hear all 39 of them. Four hundred years ago I think we went to *hear* a play; today we often go to *see* a play. In the staged reading format of the Festival, we heard these plays as if for the first time. The blend of Shakespeare with another writer was seamless and jarring at the same time. Countless actors and audience members told us that the plays were understandable in ways they had never been before.

Now it's time to share the work. We were thrilled when Ayanna Thompson and her colleagues at the Arizona Center for Medieval and Renaissance Studies offered to publish the translations for us.

I ask that you think of these as marking a moment in time.

The editions published in this series are based on the scripts that were used in the Play on! Festival in 2019. For the purpose of the readings, there were cuts allowed and these scripts represent those reading drafts.

The original commission tasked the playwrights and dramaturg to translate the whole play. The requirement of the commission was for two drafts which is enough to put the ball in play. The real fun with these texts is when there are actors, a director, a dramaturg, and the playwright wrestling with them together in a rehearsal room.

The success of a project of this scale depends on the collaboration and contributions of many people. The playwrights and dramaturgs took the assignment seriously and earnestly and were humble and gracious throughout the development of the translations. Sally Cade Holmes and Holmes Productions, our producer since the beginning, provided a steady and calm influence.

We have worked with more than 1,200 artists in the development of these works. We have partnered with more than three dozen theaters and schools. Numerous readings and more than a dozen productions of these translations have been heard and seen in the United States as well as Canada, England, and the Czech Republic.

There is a saying in the theater that 80% of the director's job is taken care of when the production is cast well. Such was my luck when I hired Taylor Bailey, who has overseen every reading and workshop, and was the producer of the Festival in New York. Katie Kennedy has gathered all the essays, and we have been supported by the rest of the Play on Shakespeare team: Kamilah Long, Summer Martin, and Amrita Ramanan.

All of this has come to be because Bill Rauch, then artistic director of the Oregon Shakespeare Festival, said yes when Dave

Hitz pitched the idea to him in 2011. Actually he said, "Hmm, interesting," which I translated to "yes." I am dearly indebted to that 'yes.'

My gratitude to Dave, Ken, and the Hitz Foundation can never be fully expressed. Their generosity, patience, and unwavering belief in what we are doing has given us the confidence to follow the advice of Samuel Beckett: "Ever tried. Ever failed. No matter. Try again. Fail again. Fail better."

Play on!

Dr. Lue Douthit
CEO/Creative Director at Play on Shakespeare
October 2020

WHAT WAS I THINKING?

On a Translation of *Titus Andronicus* ...
by Amy Freed

In 2015, Lue Douthit, the Dramaturg of the Oregon Shakespeare festival, approached me with an unusual proposition. There was a big project underway, and she had been put in charge of it. The goal was to commission what she termed "Translations" of all of Shakespeare's plays. The purpose was to make them more comprehensible to a modern audience, in real time, in performance.

The idea of a translation stopped me. A great poet, and Shakespeare was surely one of the greatest, translates *us,* by putting into words what we always knew but could never express. Who would want to interfere with Shakespeare's sound, his sense, his mind, or his mastery? Who would have the impudence to paraphrase or graft themselves onto him, even slightly? And yet . . . it is undeniable that many of the plays are hard or impossible for an uninitiated audience.

There's a real need, one that's growing greater by the year. As an educator in a theater department, I see it. I recently ran an experiment on my acting students who work on Shakespeare performance skills with me. I did it to help exorcise any sense of shame or anxiety they may have had about their comprehension level. We read the beginning of *Macbeth* out loud, and I asked them to put a hand up when they didn't understand what had been said. The hands began to go up five lines in. They were all in the air at twenty. Where then, does that leave our audiences?

The famous speeches are one thing. We've heard those words.

We are prepared for them. They have their own cultural life. But the whole of a play can be really difficult, and I wanted to understand why.

I know these translations are called Modern English. But I'm modern, I speak English, and I think that Modern English can mean almost anything. In my version of *Titus Andronicus,* I left eighty percent of the text exactly alone. That means roughly twenty percent was in some way amended. My philosophy was that if a word change was needed to help the point of a scene to land, I made it. If a construction felt clunky or obscure, so that a line's drama, impact, or speed was lost, I revised it. These changes are small, but, cumulatively, they're like cleaning one's glasses. The actor can play these thoughts and moments cleaner, and the audience finds they are feeling rather smarter than they thought.

Here's an example of my process in result.

SHAKESPEARE (unamended):
MARCUS:
Princes, that strive by factions and by friends
Ambitiously for rule and empery
Know that the people of Rome, for whom we stand
A special party, have by common voice,
In election for the Roman Empery
Chosen Andronicus, surnamed Pius;
For many good and great deserts to Rome

That speech, powerfully placed at the beginning of the play, is meant to get the dramatic stakes laid in quickly. It establishes the play's viewpoint and works quickly and powerfully to set up the crisis for the audience.

Yet some things land a little off for us. "Ambition" is a reproach here, but ambition is a virtue in modern America. "Empery" is just strange enough that we can't quite be sure what it means, although we know it certainly sounds emperor-ish. Does that blurriness help the dramatic action? "A special party?" Sounds like an orgy. He, Marcus, means he represents a body of *citizens*, not fancy princes. That is one of the most important points in the play.

> *The people have*
> *Chosen Andronicus, surnamed Pius:*
> *For many good and great deserts to Rome.*

There is something charming about the way some of Shakespeare's lines can invoke utterly wrong and weird images—in this case, the idea that Andronicus has introduced the pie to Rome, a notion that could be seriously supported by any scholar familiar with the end of the play. Still, I thought that ease of delivery and ease of comprehension would keep the velocity, lose nothing and fit right in.

Here's my version:

> *Princes that strive by factions and by friends*
> *So ambitiously to rule the Empire*
> *Know the citizens for whom I stand*
> *Representative, do by common voice*
> *In election for the Imperial throne*
> *Choose Andronicus, called Pius, so named*
> *For services to Rome both good and great*

So that is how I went about it.

∾

Along the way, I found the play to be extraordinarily fascinating. It is great and terrible in fits and starts. Like the world it describes, it is beset by disorder, unclean breaks, falls into horrible holes, and extraordinary strokes of brilliance.

Rhetoric in *Titus Andronicus* is not just a means of the play, but a big part of its subject. To write about Rome, in Shakespeare's time, was to write about the nature of oratory. In addition to developing one's own classical chops, which young Shakespeare was surely doing, his observations about the functions of high speech, placed in the mouths of his characters, are striking. They tell us about the *uses* of lamentation — and in that, make a primal case for some of the oldest meanings of art. Allegory, metaphor, and the highest flights of figure are presented within the play as a stoic's methodology for containing pain and restraining madness.

There are a lot of obvious parallels in *Titus Andronicus* and *King Lear*, although they are very different plays. Lear abandons meter and form at the outer edges of his sanity. And Titus finds it. The difference of essence is enormous between Titus' anguish poured out to a stone and Lear's storm speech: The first is a victory of poetry over brutality and the second demonstrates poetry's defeat. Lear's story is a masochistic psycho-drama where his words fail, and he finally gives way to pre-linguistic howling. Titus, by contrast, *starts* the play in a world of pre-linguistic primitivism — he's a tired-out, used-up killing machine, who only finds his voice as a human being when his dearest child is mutilated and returned to him.

Titus Andronicus operates on a compelling elemental and mythic plane. Alongside of that, its crude theatrics and manic grotesquery seem to come from an entirely different level of development — both going on in one playwright at this stage of his career.

It's impossible to know the various ingredients that went into the play's original impulses. But one thing is sure about this glorious mess of High and Low — it's a page turner, and it flies by with ferocity and speed. In spending time in close quarters with it, I saw it as both more difficult and more exciting as a theatrical prospect: Lavinia, the virtuous, is without any particularity of character. Tamora, the evil one, is a great role to play. Lucius, the noble, is a stiff. Aaron, the villain, is clearly the lead. The play is on fire whenever he's on-stage.

Titus loses us completely if we think of him as a real person who kills his son in front of us and forgets him immediately. We have to register how to see the reality of this play on multiple levels, some human, some not. That is not an easy thing to inflect through the vision of a production as a whole. But this game is worth the candle. It's fantastic, in the true sense, and a piece of art. And my hope is that in this translation — in which, I believe, my own work is quite invisible, except in those few places where it's as bold as it needs to be — this might be a production script that could help give this extraordinary play an even faster track on which to run.

∼

A final note: I've left the racist language of the original text untouched when in the mouths of the white speakers where it serves to demonstrate the forces that form and inform the tragic actions of the play. Since the author's sympathy in the play most clearly lies with Aaron, to whom Shakespeare gave the most comprehensible inner life, this language makes clear the racism that Shakespeare meant to reveal.

However, I have amended some places in Aaron's language where he inconceivably uses casual racist descriptors about himself or his child. Here Shakespeare is *not* making a theatrical choice. He's just throwing around the slurs of an era, in moments where his ear and his imagination for Aaron's reality fail him. I think he'd be glad for these small changes. If he had a chance to revise it, he would.

Amy Freed

CAST OF CHARACTERS

(in order of speaking)

SATURNINUS, the late Emperor of Rome's son

BASSIANUS, Saturninus' brother

MARCUS ANDRONICUS, Titus' brother and tribune to the people of Rome

TITUS ANDRONICUS, renowned Roman general

LUCIUS, Titus' eldest son

TAMORA, Queen of the Goths

CHIRON, Tamora's son

DEMETRIUS, Tamora's son

LAVINIA, Titus' daughter

MUTIUS, Titus' son

MARTIUS, Titus' son

QUINTUS, Titus' son

AARON, a Moor

YOUNG LUCIUS, Lucius' son and Titus' grandson

NURSE

PUBLIUS, Marcus' son

COUNTRY FELLOW

AEMILIUS, Roman noble

FIRST GOTH

SECOND GOTH

ALARBUS, Tamora's son (non-speaking role)

CAIUS, Titus' kinsmen (non-speaking role)

VALENTINE, Titus' kinsmen (non-speaking role)

SEMPRONIUS, Titus' kinsmen (non-speaking role)

Other Tribunes, Soldiers, a Roman Captain, Senators, Guards, Attendants, a Messenger, Judges, Goths, and Roman Citizens

ACT 1 ◆ SCENE 1

Flourish. Enter the Tribunes including Marcus Andronicus and
Senators aloft. And then enter, below, Saturninus and his followers
at one door, and Bassianus and his followers at another door, with
other Romans, Drums, and Trumpets.

SATURNINUS

    Noble Romans, patrons of my right
    Defend the justice of my cause with arms.
    And countrymen, my loving followers,
    Plead for my succession with your swords!
    I am the firstborn son of He the Last   5
    Who wore the imperial crown of Rome —
    So let my father's honors pass to me!
    Wrong not a firstborn's right with this indignity —

BASSIANUS

    Romans, friends, countrymen, all who follow me —
    If ever Bassianus, also Caesar's son,   10
    Found favor in the eyes of Royal Rome,
    Protect this passage to your Capitol
    And suffer no Usurper to take hold
    Of the imperial seat, to Virtue consecrate,
    To Justice, Temperance, and Nobility;   15
    But let the best in Free Election shine,
    And Romans, fight for freedom in your choice!

MARCUS

    Princes that strive by factions and by friends
    So ambitiously to rule the Empire
    Know the citizens for whom I stand   20
    Representative, do by common voice,

1

For election to the Imperial Throne,
Nominate Andronicus, Pius, so called —
For services to Rome both good and great.
A nobler man, a braver warrior,   25
Lives not this day within the city walls.
He by the Senate has been callèd home
From bitter wars against the barbarous Goths,
Who with his sons, a terror to our foes,
Has broken them that took up arms against us   30
Ten years are spent since first he undertook
This cause of Rome, and crushed our enemies' pride.
Five times he has returned bloodied to Rome,
Bearing his valiant sons in coffins from the field.
And now at last, laden with honor's spoils,   35
Returns the good Andronicus to Rome,
Renownèd Titus, victorious in war
Here let me entreat, (by honor of his name
He whom the people favor to succeed,
And in the Capital and Senate's right,   40
Which you have sworn to honor and uphold!)
That you withdraw you and reduce your strengths,
Dismiss your followers and, as suitors should,
Your reasonable cases make in peace.

SATURNINUS

How smooth this tribune speaks to calm my thoughts!   45

BASSIANUS

Marcus Andronicus, so much I place my faith
In your upright nature and integrity
So much I love and honor you and yours,
This noble brother Titus and his sons,
And her to whom my thoughts are tendered all,   50
Gracious Lavinia, Rome's bright star,

That I here do dismiss my eager friends
And for my fortunes, to the people's favor
Entrust my cause in balance to be weighed.

Bassianus' Soldiers exit

SATURNINUS

My friends who have been forward in my right,   55
I thank you all and here dismiss you all,
And to the love and favor of my country
Commit myself, my person and my cause.

Saturninus' Soldiers exit

Rome be just and gracious unto me
As I, your prince, in kind, intend to thee.   60
Open the gates and let me in!

BASSIANUS

Tribunes, and me, a poor competitor.

Flourish. They exit to go up into the Senate House.
The Tribunes and Senators exit from the upper stage
Enter a Captain

CAPTAIN

Romans, make way! The good Andronicus,
Patron of virtue, Rome's best champion,
Successful in the battles that he fights,   65
With honor and with fortune is returned
From where he did encircle by the sword —
And bend to yoke the enemies of Rome!

Sound drums and trumpets, and then enter two of Titus' sons
(Lucius and Mutius) and then two men bearing a coffin covered
with black, then two other sons (Martius and Quintus), then Titus
Andronicus, and then Tamora the Queen of Goths and her sons
Alarbus, Chiron, and Demetrius, with Aaron the Moor, and others
as many as can be, then set down the coffin, and Titus speaks.

3

TITUS

Hail Rome, victorious in your mourning weeds!
So, as the galley that unloads her freight   70
Returns with other cargo to that bay
From where she first weighed anchor and set sail —
Comes Andronicus, with laurels wreathed —
To re-salute his country — with his tears,
Tears of true joy for his return to Rome.   75
Great Jupiter, Defender of this Capitol
Sanctify those rites to which we now attend!
Romans, of my five and twenty valiant sons,
Behold the poor remains, alive and dead.
These that survive let Rome reward with love;   80
For those that I bring unto their longest home,
With burial amongst their ancestors,
Here Gods have gi'n me leave to sheathe my sword.
Titus, unkind and careless of your own,
Why suffer you your sons, unburied yet   85
To hover by the dreadful river's shore?
Make way and lay them by their brethren.

(they open the tomb)

There greet in silence, as the dead are wont,
And sleep in peace, slain in your country's wars.
O sacred receptacle of my joys,   90
Sweet cell of virtue and nobility,
How many sons have you of mine in store,
That you will never render to me more!

LUCIUS

Give us the noblest prisoner of the Goths! —
That we may tear his limbs and on a pyre,   95
To our brothers' spirits, sacrifice his flesh
Ad manes fratrum! Here —

4

Before this earthly prison of their bones,
So that their Shadows, being satisfied,
Walk not the earth to trouble us above. 100

TITUS

I give to you, the best of them that live,
The eldest son of this distressèd queen.

TAMORA

Stay, Roman brethren! — Gracious Conqueror,
Victorious Titus, see the tears I shed,
A mother's tears of anguish for her son. 105
And if your sons were ever dear to thee,
O know my son to be as dear to me.
Is not enough that we are dragged to Rome
To glorify your triumphs and return
Captive to you and to the Roman yoke, 110
But must my sons be slaughtered in the streets
For deeds done as yours did for their country?
O if to fight for king and commonwealth
Were courage in your sons, than so in mine!

(she kneels)

Andronicus, stain not your tomb with blood. 115
Would you draw near the nature of the gods?
Be like them then in being merciful.
Sweet mercy is the mark of noble nature —
Thrice-noble Titus, spare my firstborn son!

TITUS

Make ready, Ma'am, and pardon me. 120
These are the brothers left alive of those
That yours did slay. And for those brothers slain
Religiously, they ask a sacrifice.
To this your son is marked and die he must.
To appease their thirsty spirits that are gone. 125

LUCIUS

Away with him, and make a fire straight!

And with our swords we'll hack and hew his limbs

Then throw them on the pyre till they're consumed.

Exit Titus' sons with Alarbus

TAMORA *(rising and speaking to her sons)*

No Religion — Sacrilege! Alarbus!

CHIRON *(aside to Tamora and Demetrius)*

And they call us Barbarians! —   130

DEMETRIUS *(aside to Tamora and Chiron)*

Alarbus goes to his rest while we live

To tremble under Titus' threat'ning look.

So Madam, show nothing. And hope the Gods

May yet arm Tamora, who was the Queen of Goths!   135

(When Goths were Goths and Tamora was Queen)

To requite these bloody wrongs upon her foes.

Enter the sons of Andronicus again with bloody swords

LUCIUS

See, Lord and father, how we have performed

Our Roman Rites. Alarbus' limbs are lopped,

His entrails feed the sacrificing fire,   140

His smoke like incense does perfume the sky.

Nothing now remains but to inter our brothers.

So let our trumpets welcome them back home.

TITUS

Let it be so. And let Andronicus

Make this his last farewell unto their souls.   145

Sound Trumpets! Place their coffins in the tomb.

In peace and honor rest you here, my sons,

Rome's Ready Champions, here find your repose

Safe from the world's chances and mishaps.

No sound, but silence and eternal sleep.   150

In peace and honor rest you here, my sons.

Enter Lavinia

LAVINIA

In peace and honor live Lord Titus long;

My noble Lord and Father, live in fame.

(she kneels)

Lo, at this tomb I pay those tears I owe

Rendered to my brothers, due their rites.   155

But at these feet I kneel, with tears of joy

Shed on living earth for this return.

O bless me here, with your victorious hand,

Whose fortunes Rome's best citizens applaud.

TITUS

Kind Rome, have you thus lovingly preserved   160

This sweetness of mine age to glad my heart!

Lavinia, live long, outlive your father's days

And may your Virtue's name outlive all mortal praise.

Lavinia rises

Enter Marcus Andronicus, carrying a white robe

Enter aloft Saturninus, Bassianus, Tribunes, Senators, and Guards

MARCUS

Long live Lord Titus, my beloved brother,

Gracious and triumphant in the eyes of Rome!   165

TITUS

Thanks, Gentle Tribune, noble brother Marcus.

MARCUS

And welcome, nephews, from successful wars —

You that survive, and those that sleep in fame.

Alive or dead, the honor is alike for all

That in your country's service drew your swords;   170

But safer honor lies in funeral pomp

For call no man happy who is not dead

7

And triumphs over chance in honor's bed.
Titus Andronicus, the people of Rome,
Whose friend in justice you have ever been,   175
Send you by me, their tribune and their trust,
A Candidate's robe of white and spotless hue
And name you in election for the empire
With these our late-deceasèd emperor's sons.
Be Candidate, then, and put it on,   180
And help to set a head on headless Rome.

TITUS

A better head her glorious body fits
Than his that shakes for age and feebleness.

(to Tribunes and Senators aloft)

What, how should I don this robe and serve you?   185
To be chosen and proclaimed today,
Tomorrow yield up rule, resign the role,
And leave a host of troubles for you all?
Rome, I have been your soldier forty years,
And led my country's strength successfully,   190
And buried one and twenty valiant sons,
Knighted in war's heat, slain manfully in arms,
In right and service of their noble country.
Give me a staff of honor for mine age,
But not a scepter to control the world.   195
Upright he held it, lords, that held it last.

MARCUS

Titus, you shall have, if ask, the empire.

SATURNINUS

Proud and ambitious tribune, say you so?

TITUS

Patience, Prince Saturninus.

SATURNINUS

    Romans, do me right!   200

    Patricians, draw your swords and sheathe them not

    Till Saturninus be Rome's emperor. —

    Andronicus, better you were shipped to hell

    Than rob me of the people's hearts.

LUCIUS

    Proud Saturnine, you interrupt the good   205

    That noble-minded Titus means to you.

TITUS

    (Content you, prince, I'll wean the people's hearts

    From me and to you I will restore them.)

BASSIANUS

    Andronicus, I do not flatter you,

    But honor you, and will do till I die.   210

    If you'll my faction strengthen with your friends,

    I will most thankful be, and thanks to men

    Of noble minds, is thanks enough.

TITUS

    People of Rome, and people's tribunes here,

    I ask of you your voices and your votes.   215

    Where Andronicus bids, will you bestow them?

TRIBUNES

    To gratify the good Andronicus

    In joy that he is safe returned to Rome,

    The people will accept whom he will choose.

TITUS

    Tribunes, I thank you; then this suit I ask: 220

    That you will our emperor's eldest son elect,

    Lord Saturnine, whose virtues will, I know,

    Reflect on Rome as bright as Sun on Earth

    And ripen justice in this commonwealth.

Then, if you will select by my advice,   225

Crown him and say "Long live our emperor."

MARCUS

Highborn men and low alike we make

Lord Saturninus Rome's great Emperor,

And cry "Long live our Emperor Saturnine."

A long flourish till Saturninus, Bassianus,

and Guards come down

SATURNINUS

Titus Andronicus, for your duties done   230

For us in our election on this day,

I thank you for but part of what I owe

My deeds will pay the rest of your true service.

And to begin, Titus, to elevate

Your name and honorable family,   235

Lavinia will I take to be my empress,

Rome's royal mistress, mistress of my heart,

And will wed her in the sacred Pantheon.

So I do "propose." Art pleased? How say you,

(Lavinia goes to speak —)

Titus?   240

TITUS

I do, my lord, accept. And in this match

I am most highly honored of your Grace;

And here before all Rome, to Saturnine,

King and commander of our commonwealth,

The wide world's emperor, do I lay down   245

My sword, my chariot, and my prisoners.

Worthy gifts for Rome's imperious lord.

Receive them then, these tributes that I owe

Mine honor's emblems, humbled at your feet.

SATURNINUS

    Noble Titus, father of my crown and Bride.   250

    How proud I am of you and of your gifts,

    Rome shall record. And if ever I forget

    The least of your deeds, feats too great for speech —

    Romans, forget your fealty to me.

TITUS *(to Tamora)*

    Now, madam, I give you to an Emperor,   255

    To him that for your honor and your state

    Will use you nobly, and your followers.

SATURNINUS

    (A goodly lady, trust me, of that flavor

    I would favor, were I to do it over —)

    Clear up, fair queen, that stormy countenance   260

    Though war's misfortunes wrought this change of fate,

    You'll not to be made a scorn in Rome.

    For I shall use thee princely. Every way.

    Trust this comfort, let not your grief dash hope.

    I can make you greater than the Queen of Goths. —   265

    So be not Gauled.

    Lavinia, you aren't displeased, I hope?

LAVINIA

    Why no, my lord, the courtesy of princes

    Demands such words of true nobility.

SATURNINUS

    Thanks, sweet Lavinia. — Romans, let us go.   270

    And now we do proclaim our prisoners free!

    Announce us, lords, with trumpet and with drum.

        Flourish. Saturninus and his Guards exit, with Drums and

            Trumpets. Tribunes and Senators exit aloft.

BASSIANUS

    Lord Titus, by your leave, this maid is mine.

TITUS

How, sir? Are you in earnest then, my lord?

BASSIANUS

Ay, noble Titus. And I will tell you here   275

I have both right and reason on my side.

TITUS

By what reason and what right!

BASSIANUS

My reason? — That I've made her mine.

"To each his own."

Bassianus takes Lavinia by the arm

MARCUS

Ah. "*Suum cuique!*" It is our Roman Justice.   280

This prince, in justice, "seizes what is his."

LUCIUS

And that he will and shall, if Lucius live!

TITUS

Traitors! Where is the Emperor's guard?

Enter Saturninus and his Guards

Treason, my lord! Lavinia is taken!

SATURNINUS

Taken? By whom?   285

BASSIANUS

By the man that might with justice on his side

From another tear away his bride!

MUTIUS

Brothers, help him to quickly bear her hence,

And with my sword I'll hold the door.

Bassianus, Lavinia, Marcus, Lucius, Quintus, and Martius exit

TITUS *(to Saturninus)*

Follow, my lord, and I'll soon bring her back.   290

Saturninus, Tamora, Demetrius, Chiron, Aaron, and Guards exit

12

MUTIUS

My lord, you pass not here.

TITUS

What, villain boy,

Bar me my way in Rome?

He stabs Mutius

MUTIUS

Help, Lucius, help!

Mutius dies

Enter Lucius

LUCIUS

My lord — what have you done! Oh, Injustice!   295

Have you in mad mistaking slain your son!

TITUS

Not you nor he are any sons of mine.

My sons would never so dishonor me.

Traitor, restore Lavinia to the Emperor.

Enter aloft the Emperor Saturninus

with Tamora and her two sons and Aaron the Moor

LUCIUS

Dead, if you will! But never as his wife.   300

She is another's lawful promised love.

He exits

SATURNINUS

No, Titus, no, the Emperor needs her not,

Not her, nor you, nor any of your stock.

Mock me once, I'll trust awhile. But twice?

Never, nor your traitorous haughty sons,   305

Confederates all — to thus dishonor me!

Was there none in Rome to make your fool

But Saturnine? Full well, Andronicus,

These deeds agree with that proud boast of yours

That said I begged the empire at your hands. 310
TITUS
O monstrous! What reproachful words are these?
SATURNINUS
But go your ways. And give that piece of work
To him that pulled his sword for her.
A valiant son-in-law you shall enjoy,
One fit to riot with your lawless sons, 315
And rumble in the commonwealth of Rome.
TITUS
These words are razors to my wounded heart.
SATURNINUS *(to Tamora)*
And therefore, Radiant Tamora, Queen of Goths,
Who as the Lunar Goddess 'mongst her nymphs
Outshines our Lovely Roman Ladies, 320
If you approve my sudden swings of mood,
I choose you, Tamora, for my bride
And will create you Empress of Rome.
Speak, Queen of Goths, if this does please,
And I will swear by all the Roman Gods, 325
(Since priest and holy water are at hand,
And tapers burn so bright, and everything
In readiness for the rites of Marriage stands)
I will not greet these Roman streets again
Or in the palace take my place till forth 330
I lead my lawful wedded bride along with me.
TAMORA
And here in sight of heaven, to Rome I swear,
If Saturnine shall lift the Queen of Goths,
She will be handmaid to his all-desires,
And loving nurse, and mother to his youth. 335

SATURNINUS

    Then ascend, Fair Queen, to Pantheon. —

    Lords, accompany your noble emperor

    And at his side this lovely bride,

    By heaven sent for Prince Saturnine,

    Whose wisdom has her fortunes overcome.   340

    There shall we consummate. And after, marry.

Exit

TITUS

    He asks not me — to wait upon this bride.

    Titus, when were you left to walk alone,

    Dishonored thus and thus of wrongs accused —

Enter Marcus and Titus' sons, Lucius, Martius, and Quintus

MARCUS

    O Titus, see! O See what you have done!   345

    In your anger slain a virtuous son!

TITUS

    No, foolish tribune, no; no son of mine,

    Nor are you my brother, confederates with these —

    That have dishonored all our family.

    Unworthy brother and unworthy sons!   350

LUCIUS

    Let us give him burial as becomes him.

    Give Mutius burial with our brethren.

TITUS

    Traitors, away! He rests not in this tomb.

    This monument five hundred years has stood,

    Whose outer walls are shored with stone   355

    And inner with the bones of my true sons.

    Here none but soldiers and Rome's servitors

    Repose in fame, no base brawlers and so slain.

    Bury him where you can. He comes not here.

15

MARCUS

My lord, this is profanity in you.   360

My nephew Mutius' deeds do plead for him.

He must be buried with his brethren.

MARTIUS

And shall, or him we'll accompany.

TITUS

"And Shall"? What villain dares to speak those words?

MARTIUS

He that would enforce it any place but here.   365

TITUS

What, would you bury him in spite of me?

MARCUS

No, noble Titus, but we beg of you

To pardon Mutius and to bury him.

TITUS

Marcus, you have struck me to the quick,

And with these boys mine honor you have hurt.   370

My enemies you are, and I rebuke you.

Now trouble me no more, and get you gone.

QUINTUS

He is not himself; let us withdraw.

MARTIUS

I will not, till Mutius' bones be buried.

                    Marcus, Lucius, Martius, and Quintus kneel

MARCUS

Brother, for in that name does nature plead —   375

MARTIUS

Father, and in that name does nature speak —

TITUS

Speak no more lest you do speak your last.

16

MARCUS

Renowned Titus, more than half my soul —

LUCIUS

Dear father, soul and substance of us all —

MARCUS

Suffer thy brother Marcus leave to place   380

His noble nephew here in honor's nest,

He died in honor and Lavinia's cause.

You are a Roman; be not barbarous.

Let not young Mutius, then, that was your joy,

Be barred his entrance here.   385

TITUS

Rise, Marcus, rise.

(they rise)

The darkest day is this that e'er I saw,

To be dishonored by my sons in Rome.

Well. Bury him, and bury me the next.

They put Mutius in the tomb

LUCIUS

There lie thy bones, sweet Mutius, with thy friends',   390

Till with soldier's honors we adorn thy tomb.

(they all except Titus kneel and say)

No man shed tears for noble Mutius

Dulce et decorum est pro patria mori.

All but Marcus and Titus exit

MARCUS

My lord, to step out of these dreary dumps —

How comes it that the subtle Queen of Goths   395

Is so suddenly risen in Rome?

TITUS

I know not, Marcus, but I know it is.

Whether by design or not, heavens knows.

17

But is she not now beholden to the man
That lifted her unto this royal turn?   400
Yes, and, oh, she will royally him repay.

Enter the Emperor Saturninus, Tamora,
and her two sons, with the Moor.

At another door, Bassianus and Lavinia, with Titus' three sons.

SATURNINUS

So, Bassianus, you've made off with the prize.
God give you joy, sir, of your gallant bride.

BASSIANUS

And you of yours, my lord. I say no more,
Nor wish no less, and so I take my leave.   405

SATURNINUS

Traitor, if Rome have law or we have power,
You and your faction shall repent this rape.

BASSIANUS

"Rape"! Call rescue? What? To seize my own,
My true betrothéd love and now my wife?
Well, let the laws of Rome determine all.   410
Meanwhile am I possessed of what is mine.

SATURNINUS

Well done, sir, you are very short with us.
But if we live, we'll be as sharp with you.

BASSIANUS

My lord, what I have done, as best I may,
Answer I must, and shall do with my life.   415
But this I give your Grace to know —
By all the duties that I owe to Rome,
This noble gentleman, Lord Titus here,
Is in your opinion and in honor wronged!
For in the rescue of Lavinia   420
In your fierce defense, and moved to wrath

18

That could not be controlled
With his own hand did slay his youngest son.
Receive him then to favor, Saturnine,
That has revealed himself in all his deeds   425
A father and a friend to you and Rome.

TITUS

Prince Bassianus, plead not you my deeds.
'Tis you, and these, that have dishonored me.
Rome and righteous heavens be my judge
How I have loved and honored Saturnine.   430

He kneels

TAMORA *(to Saturninus)*

My worthy lord, if ever Tamora
Found favor in those princely eyes of thine,
Let one new to all speak fairly for each,
And at my suit, sweet, Pardon what is past.

SATURNINUS

What, Madam, be openly dishonored,   435
And cravenly put up without revenge?

TAMORA

Not so, my Lord; the Roman Gods forbid
I should advocate for your dishonor.
But on mine honor, here, I dare proclaim
For good Lord Titus' innocence in all,   440
His uncontrolled fury shows his griefs.
Then at my suit look mercifully on him.
Lose not a noble friend on false surmise,
Nor with bitter looks afflict his gentle heart.

(aside to Saturninus)

My lord, be ruled by me; this game is long.   445
Hide your grudges and your discontents —
You are but newly planted in your throne —

19

Lest common people and patricians both,
Upon reflection take up Titus' part
And then uproot you for ingratitude, 450
Which Rome regards to be a primal sin.
Yield at my entreats, and then turn me loose.
I'll find a day to massacre them all
And raze their faction and their family,
The cruel father and his traitorous sons, 455
To whom I cried for my dear son's life,
And make them feel what 'tis to let a queen
Kneel in the streets and beg for grace in vain.
(aloud)
Come, come, Sweet Emperor — Come, Andronicus —
Take up this good old man, and cheer the heart 460
That dies in the tempest of your angry frown.

SATURNINUS

Rise, Titus, rise. My Empress has prevailed.

TAMORA

Titus, although I am but new in Rome,
I find myself most happily at home,
And will advise my Emperor for his good. 465
This day all quarrels die, Andronicus.
And let it be mine honor, good my lord,
If I may reconcile your friends and you.
For you, Prince Bassianus, I have made
My word and promise to the Emperor 470
You will no troubles make from here on out.
And fear not, lords — nor you, Lavinia.
(But I do think it might be wise, that you should
Humbly on your knees, ask pardon of his Majesty.)
        Marcus, Lavinia, Lucius, Martius, and Quintus kneel

LUCIUS

    We do, and swear to heaven and to his highness   475

    That what we did was only what was right,

    To protect our sister's honor and our own.

MARCUS

    That, on mine honor, here do I affirm.

SATURNINUS

    Away, and talk not; trouble us no more.

TAMORA

    Nay, Nay, Sweet Emperor, let us all be friends.   480

    See how they all kneel to you for grace.

    I will not be denied, Sweetheart, come back.

SATURNINUS

    Marcus, for your sake and your brother's here,

    And at my lovely Tamora's entreats,

    I will forgive these young men's heinous faults.   485

    Get up.

(they rise)

    Lavinia, though you left me like a churl,

    I found a treasure, and sure as death I swore

    I would not part a bachelor from the priest.

    Come, if the Emperor's court can feast two brides,   490

    You are my guest, Lavinia, and your friends. —

    This day shall be a love-day, Tamora.

TITUS

    Tomorrow, and it please your Majesty

    To hunt the Panther and the Deer with me,

    We'll sound the horns and loudly bay   495

    And greet your Grace as soon as breaks the day.

SATURNINUS

    Be it so, Titus, and scarcely can we wait.

                Sound trumpets. All but Aaron exit

ACT 2 ◆ SCENE 1

AARON *(alone)*

Now climbs Tamora to Olympus' top,
Safe from Fortune's shot, and sits aloft,
Secure from thunder's crack or lightning flash,
Advanced above the threat'ning reach of men.
And as the golden sun salutes the morn   5
As first he gilds the ocean with his beams,
Then climbs the heavens in his glistening coach
And paints with flame the highest mountain streams
So Tamora, on high, is touched by fire.
Upon her now do earthly honors wait,   10
And virtue sinks and trembles at her frown.
So, Aaron, arm your heart and fit your thoughts
And with your royal mistress mount the heights
To her degree who long has lovèd me,
Who hath her fettered in amorous chains.   15
More bound than Prometheus to his rock
Is she in bondage to my eyes — and — Now!
Away with slave-like garments, servile thoughts!
I will be bright and shine in pearl and gold
To wait upon this new-made empress.   20
To wait, said I? To wanton with this queen,
This goddess, this historic whore, this nymph,
This siren that will charm Rome's Saturnine
And see his ship wreck and his country's ruin.
Hello! What storm is this?   25

Enter Chiron and Demetrius, scuffling

23

DEMETRIUS

Chiron, you lack in years, you want for wits —
And manners! You intrude where I intend to go —
And may for all that you know — stand a chance!

CHIRON

Demetrius, you overbear in all,
Is it your plan to bury me in bragging? 30
Think you our difference of a year or two
Makes me less a man and you more pleasing?
I am as able and as fit as you
To serve and to deserve a lady's favor,
And with my sword, I prove it on you! 35
And will plead my passions for Lavinia's love.

AARON *(aside)*

Blows! Brawls! These lovers will not keep the peace.

DEMETRIUS *(to Chiron)*

Why, Boy, although our mother, ill-advised,
Gave you a little wooden sword to wear,
Are you grown so desperate to wave it at your friends? 40
Go to. Have your toy glued within your sheath
Till you know better how to handle it.

CHIRON

Meanwhile, Sir, with the little skill I have,
Full well shalt feel how much I dare.

DEMETRIUS

Ay, Boy, Grow you so brave? 45

They draw

AARON

Why, how now, lords?
So near the Emperor's palace dare you draw
And openly break into such a quarrel?
Full well I know the reason for your fight.

And I would not for a pot of gold   50
This should reach the ears of those it concerns,
Nor for more would I have your noble mother
Be dishonored in the eyes of Rome.
For shame! Put up.

DEMETRIUS

Not I, till I have sheathed   55
My rapier in his bosom, and then I'll
Thrust those insulting speeches down his throat
That he dares breath in my dishonor here.

CHIRON

Oh, I am prepared and full resolved,
Foul-spoken coward, who thunders with your tongue   60
And no action with your weapon dare perform.

AARON

Away, I say!
Now by those gods you warlike Goths adore,
This petty scuffle will undo us all.
Why, lords, do you know how dangerous   65
It is to steal upon a prince's right?
What, is Lavinia now become so loose
Or Bassianus so degenerate
That for her love such quarrels can be broached —
And bring not justice down upon on your heads?   70
Young lords, beware! For should the Empress know
The source of this discord, that music would not please.

CHIRON

I care not, let her know! She and all the world.
I love Lavinia more than all the world.

DEMETRIUS

Youngling, learn to make some plainer choice.   75
Lavinia is your elder brother's hope.

AARON

    Are you two mad? Know not you are in Rome?

    And what Italians are, jealous and hot

    And cannot have competitors in love?

    I tell you, lords, you guarantee your deaths   80

    By this desire.

CHIRON

    Aaron, a thousand deaths

    I'd die if I could have her whom I love.

AARON

    To have her how?

DEMETRIUS

    Why make you it so strange?   85

    She is a woman, therefore may be wooed;

    She is a woman, therefore may be won;

    She is Lavinia, therefore must be loved.

    What, man, more water glides by the mill

    Than the miller sees, and how easy 'tis,   90

    Once the loaf is cut, to steal a piece, we know.

    Though Bassianus be the Emperor's brother

    Better than he have "worn the horns" as Vulcan did!

CHIRON

    Huh?

DEMETRIUS

    — When Mars was in Venus.   95

                Brothers laugh

AARON *(aside)*

    Ay and one as high as Saturninus may.

DEMETRIUS

    Then why should I despair? I know to woo

    With words, fair looks, and liberality.

    What, have we all not often shot a doe

And stolen her away beneath the keeper's nose?   100

AARON

Why then it seems to take one certain shot
Would serve your turn.

CHIRON

Ay, so the turn were served.

DEMETRIUS

Aaron, you have hit it.

AARON

Would that you had hit it too — for then   105
You would not be such fools to fight for this.
What if both your turns were served at once? —
Too much?

CHIRON

Faith, not for me.

DEMETRIUS

Nor me, if one of the both.   110

AARON

For shame, be friends, and join for which you joust.
For policy and strategy can do
What you desire, but first you must accept
You cannot, singly, have as you would —
So hunt together, and take what you can.   115
For know of me; Lucrece was not more chaste
Than this Lavinia, Bassianus' love.
A quicker course than ling'ring longing
Must we pursue, and I have found the path.
My lords, a hunting party is in hand;   120
There will roam the lovely Roman ladies.
The forest walks are wide and soft,
And many lonely paths there are,
Fitted by kind for rape and villainy.

27

Corner her there, this dainty doe,   125
Then, strike her home by force, forget your words.
This the way, or none, stand you to be relieved.
Come, Come, our empress, with her highest arts
To villainy for vengeance consecrated,
Will we at once acquaint of our intent,   130
And she shall refine the outline of our plot
Not suffer you to like animals contend
But hunt together to advance desire's end.
The Emperor's court is like a house of Glass,
The palace full of tongues, of eyes, and ears;   135
The woods are ruthless, dreadful, deaf and dull.
There speak and strike, brave boys, and take your turns.
There serve your lust, shadowed from heaven's eye,
And revel in Lavinia's treasury.

CHIRON

This counsel, Boy, is not for cowards.   140

DEMETRIUS

Right or wrong, till I find that stream
To cool this heat, a charm to calm these fits,
I am on fire.

They exit

ACT 2 ◆ SCENE 2

Enter Titus Andronicus and his three sons, and Marcus making a
noise with hounds and horns

TITUS

The hunt is up, and so is yet the moon,
The fields are fragrant and the woods glow green.
Unleash the dogs and set them all to bay!
Awake the Emperor and his lovely bride
And rouse the Prince, as now we wind the horns   5

And shake the sleeping court with hunter's peal.
Sons, let it be your care, as it is mine,
To attend the Emperor's person watchfully.
For I was troubled in my sleep this night,
But the dawning day some comfort brings me.   10

A cry of hounds, and horns in a peal. Then enter Saturninus,
Tamora, Bassianus, Lavinia, Chiron, Demetrius, and their
Attendants.

TITUS

Many good morrows to your Majesty;
Madam, to you as many, and as good.
I promised your Grace a hunter's peal.

SATURNINUS

And you have rung it lustily, my lords —
Somewhat too early for new-married ladies.   15

BASSIANUS

Lavinia, how say you?

LAVINIA

Too early, no.
We have been awake two hours and more.

SATURNINUS

Come on, then. Horse and chariots let's have,
And to the sport.   20

(to Tamora)

Madam, now you shall see
Our Roman hunting.

MARCUS

I have dogs, my lord,
Will rouse the fiercest panther from its lair
And run it to the highest mountain peak.   25

TITUS

And I have horse will follow where the game

29

Makes way and runs like swallows o'er the plain
DEMETRIUS *(aside to Chiron)*

Though we hunt not with horse nor hound,

We'll pluck that dainty doe to the ground.

They exit

ACT 2 ◆ SCENE 3

Enter Aaron, alone, carrying a bag of gold

AARON

He that had a wit would think that I had none,

To bury so much gold under a tree

And never after to reclaim it.

Let him that would think I am a fool

Know that with this gold I set a coiled trap   5

So cunningly contrived, that when it snap, will beget

A very excellent piece of villainy.

(he hides the bag)

So rest, sweet gold, for their instruction

Who'll find their wages by the empress paid.

Enter Tamora alone to Aaron the Moor

TAMORA

My lovely Aaron, why look you so sad,   10

When everything does make a joyous show?

The birds chant melody on every bush,

The snake uncoils her in the cheerful sun,

The green leaves quiver with the cooling wind

And dance their checkered shadows on the ground.   15

In this sweet hollow, Aaron, shall we rest,

And listen as the echo mocks the hounds,

Replying slyly to the well-tuned horns,

As if a double hunt were heard at once,

Let us sit and chase our pleasures down.   20

Like Dido and Aeneas — who, as story goes
Lost their way, and in the rain took shelter
In a happy cave and found their love —
So may we, wreathed in the other's arms
Our pastimes done, possess a golden slumber,   25
While hounds and horns and sweet melodious birds
Be to us as is a nurse's song
Of lullaby to make the baby sleep.

AARON

Though Venus, hot and red, rule your desire,
Tis Saturn, cold and black, that ruleth mine.   30
Can'st read the deadly power in my gaze,
My silence, my thought-thick melancholy —
My tight coiled curls that now begin to stir
Alive like the adder when she unfolds
To do some fatal execution?   35
Madam, these are none of Venus' love-signs
Vengeance is in my heart, death in my hand,
Blood and revenge are hammering in my head
Hark, Tamora, the empress of my Soul,
That wants no more of heaven than in thee,   40
This is the day of doom for Bassianus.
His Nightingale must lose her tongue today,
Your sons make a pillage of her purity,
And wash their hands in Bassianus' blood.

(he takes out a paper)

See you this letter? Take it up I pray,   45
And give the King this fatal-plotting scroll.

(he hands her the paper)

Now do not question me, we are spotted.
Here comes a part of the hoped-for parcel,
Full unaware how near destruction lies.

Enter Bassianus and Lavinia

TAMORA

    Ah, my sweet Moor, sweeter to me than life!   50

AARON

    No more, great empress. Bassianus comes.

    Provoke them, and I'll fetch your sons

    To back your quarrels, whatever you contrive.

He exits

BASSIANUS

    Well, well. If 'tis not Rome's royal empress

    Out and about without her body slave!   55

    Or is it Dian (for somewhat dressed like her)

    Who has abandoned her holy groves

    To roam the forest where the mortals hunt?

TAMORA

    Insolence! Would you command my private walks!

    Oh, Would I were your Goddess of the Hunt —   60

    I'd make forked horns shoot forth upon your head

    That your own dogs should take you for a stag

    And drag you down and tear you limb to limb,

    Rude intruder on my sacred groves.

LAVINIA

    Gentle Empress, we well believe you could   65

    'Tis known you have a goodly gift in horning —

    And 'tis like your Moor and you have ventured out

    To see if you might hang a few this morning!

    Jove shield your husband from his hounds today!

    'Tis likely they should take him for a stag!   70

BASSIANUS

    All know, Queen, your gloomy Sumerian

    Does make your honor of his body's hue

    Dark, detested, and abominable —

Why have you escaped your entourage
Uncoupled from your snow-white royal steed   75
And led a coal-black Moor to this dark glade
Had lust not led you here to do the deed?

LAVINIA

And being intercepted in your sport,
Let fly your loose abuse upon my lord!
For insolence! I pray you, let us hence.   80
Let her here enjoy her raven-colored love,
In this thicket perfect for her purpose.

BASSIANUS

The King shall know of her and the Moor —

LAVINIA

— the merrier for the king's abuse.
Oh, to use the poor emperor so!   85

TAMORA

See my patience to endure all this

Enter Chiron and Demetrius

DEMETRIUS

How now, dear Empress and gracious mother,
Why does your Highness look so pale and wan?

TAMORA

Have I not reason, think you, to look pale?
These two have lured me hither to this place,   90
A barren, horrid, hollow as you see;
The trees, though summer, are forlorn and lean,
O'ergrown with moss and baleful mistletoe.
Here never shines the sun, here nothing breeds,
Unless the nightly owl or fatal raven.   95
And as they showed me this abhorrèd pit,
They told me, at the deadly time of night
A thousand fiends, a thousands hissing snakes,

Ten thousand swelling toads, as many imps,
Do make such fearful and confused cries   100
That if any mortal body hears it
They straight fall mad, or die at once of fright.
No sooner had they told this hellish tale
But straight they told me they would bind me to
The blackened trunk of an ill-starred yew   105
And leave me to this miserable death.
And then they called me foul adulteress,
Sluttish Goth, and all the bitterest terms
That ever ear did hear to such effect.
And had you not by wondrous fortune come,   110
This vengeance on me had they executed.
Revenge it as you love your mother's life,
Or be you not henceforth called my children.

DEMETRIUS *(drawing his dagger)*

This is a witness that I am your son.

CHIRON *(drawing his dagger)*

And this for me, strike home and prove your son!   115

They stab Bassianus

LAVINIA

Oh, you ravening whore — nay, say TAMORA
For no name fits your nature but your own!

TAMORA

Give me your dagger! You shall see, my boys,
Your mother's hand shall right your mother's wrong.

DEMETRIUS

Stay, madam, we have more to do with her.   120
First let's reap the corn, then burn the husk.
This minion stands upon her purity,
Upon her marriage vows, her chastity.
And with that painted hope she dares upbraid you

34

And shall she carry that unto her grave? 125
CHIRON

And if she does, I'll geld myself in shame!

Drag her husband into some secret hole

And we'll make his dead trunk pillow to our lust.
TAMORA

But when you have the honey you desire,

Let not this wasp outlive us all to sting. 130
CHIRON

I warrant you, madam, that, we'll make sure.

Come, mistress, now by force we will enjoy

That finely-flouted purity of yours.
LAVINIA

O Tamora, thou bearest a woman's face —
TAMORA

I will not hear her speak. Away with her. 135
LAVINIA

Sweet lords, entreat her hear me but a word.
DEMETRIUS *(to Tamora)*

Listen, fair madam. Let it be your glory

To see her tears, but be your heart as hard to them

As unrelenting flint to drops of rain.
LAVINIA

When did the tiger's young ones teach the dam? 140

O, do not teach her wrath; she taught it you.

The milk you suck'st from her did turn to bile.

Even at her teat you learned her tyranny.

Yet mothers breed not every son alike.

(to Chiron)

I beg you, beg her show a woman's pity — 145
CHIRON

What, have me prove myself a bastard?

35

LAVINIA

'Tis true; the raven does not hatch a lark.
Yet have I heard — O, could I prove it true! —
The lion, moved with pity, did endure
To have his princely claws pared all away.   150
Some say that ravens foster forlorn children
While their own babies famish in their nests.
O, be to me, though your hard heart say no,
Not kind but have some little pity.

TAMORA

I know not what it means. — Away with her.   155

LAVINIA

O, let me teach thee! For my father's sake,
That gave you life when well he might have slain thee,
Be not stone; but open thy deaf ears.

TAMORA

Even had you never offered me offense,
Even for Alarbus' sake am I pitiless. —   160
Remember, boys, I poured forth tears in vain
To save your brother from the sacrifice,
But fierce Andronicus would not relent.
Therefore away with her, and use her as you will;
The worse for her, the better you love me.   165

LAVINIA

O Tamora, be called a gentle queen,
And with thine own hands kill me in this place!
For 'tis not life that I have begged so long;
For I was slain when Bassianus died.

TAMORA

What, beg you, then? Fool woman, let me go!   170

LAVINIA

To die, I beg, and one thing more

36

That womanhood denies my tongue to tell.
O, keep me from their worse-than-killing lust,
And tumble me into some loathsome pit
Where never man's eye may behold my body.   175
Do this, and be a charitable murderer.

TAMORA

So should I rob my sweet sons of their due.
No, let them satisfy their lust on you.

DEMETRIUS *(to Lavinia)*

Away, you've stayed us here too long!

LAVINIA *(to Tamora)*

No grace, no womanhood? Oh, beast! Creature!   180
The blot and enemy to our very name!
Confusion fall —

CHIRON

Nay, then, I'll stop your mouth. — Bring her husband.
This is the hole where Aaron bid us hide him.

> *They put Bassianus' body in the pit and exit,*
> *carrying off Lavinia*

TAMORA

Farewell, my sons. And see that she is silenced.   185
Ne'er let my heart know happiness indeed
Till all the Andronici be made away.
Now will I hence to seek my lovely Moor,
And let my sportful sons this slag deflower.

> *She exits*

> *Enter Aaron with two of Titus' sons, Quintus and Martius*

AARON

Come on, my lords, the better foot before.   190
Straight will I bring you to the loathsome pit
Where I espied a panther fast asleep.

QUINTUS

— Some veil has crossed my sight. Mine eyes grow dim.

MARTIUS

Mine too, I promise you. Were it not a shame

To leave our sport, I could sleep here awhile.   195

He falls into the pit

QUINTUS

What, art fallen? What secret hole is this,

Its mouth is covered with rude-growing briars

Upon its leaves are drops of new-shed blood

As fresh as morning dew distilled on flowers!

A deadly place it seems. Brother! Speak   200

Are you wounded with the fall?

MARTIUS

O, Brother, by the dismal'st sight

That ever wounded eye, made heart lament!

AARON *(aside)*

Now will I fetch the King to find them here,

And he will put these two and two together   205

And guess that it was they that killed his brother.

He exits

MARTIUS

Why do you not reach down to me and help me

From this unhallowed and bloodstained hole!

QUINTUS

I am surprisèd with unholy fear.

A chilling sweat overruns my trembling limbs.   210

My heart suspects more than mine eye can see.

MARTIUS

To prove indeed a true-divining heart,

Aaron and you look down into this den

And see a fearful sight of blood and death.

38

QUINTUS

Aaron is gone, and my apprehensive heart 215
Will not permit me cast mine eyes and see
The thing it trembles to imagine.
O, tell me who it is, for not till now
Was I a child to fear I know not what.

MARTIUS

Lord Bassianus lies betrayed in blood, 220
All on a heap, like to a slaughtered lamb,
In this detested, dark, blood-drinking hole.

QUINTUS

How can you be sure in such a darkness?

MARTIUS

Upon his bloody finger he does wear
A ring that has a gleaming gem 225
Which like a taper in a catacomb,
Doth shine upon the dead man's earthy cheeks
And lights the ragged entrails of the vault.
So pale did shine the moon on Pyramus
When he lay dead and drenched in blood and night. 230
O, brother, help me with thy shaking hand —
If fear hath made thee faint as it makes me —
Out! Out of this fell devouring chamber
As hateful as the mouth of misty hell.

QUINTUS *(reaching into the pit)*

Reach me thy hand, so I may pull thee out 235
And, if lacking strength enough to save thee
I'll plunge to join thee in the swallowing womb
Of this deep pit, poor Bassianus' Grave.

(he pulls Martius' hand)

I have no strength to pull thee to the brink.

MARTIUS

Nor I no strength to climb without thy help. 240

QUINTUS

Your hand again. Once more. I will not let go

Till you are here above or I below. Hold!

You cannot come to me. I come to you.

He falls in. Enter the Emperor Saturninus,
with Attendants, and Aaron the Moor.

SATURNINUS

Come all! Along with me! We'll see this hole

And what he is that now leaps into it. — 245

Say, who is it that hastily descends

Into this gaping hollow of the earth?

MARTIUS

The unhappy sons of old Andronicus

Brought hither in a most unlucky hour

To find your brother Bassianus dead. 250

SATURNINUS

My brother dead! A lie — a brutal jest —

I left him with his lady at the lodge

Upon the north side of our hunting ground.

'Tis not an hour since I left them there.

MARTIUS

You may have left them there alive, 255

But here we have found him slain.

Enter Tamora, Titus Andronicus, and Lucius

TAMORA

Where is my lord the King?

SATURNINUS

Here, Tamora, and wracked with killing grief.

TAMORA

Where is your brother Bassianus?

SATURNINUS

Now to the bottom do you probe my wound.   260

Poor Bassianus here lies murdered.

TAMORA

Then too late I bring this fatal page,

The plot by which this tragedy was played,

And wonder greatly that a man's face can

In pleasing smiles wrap such murd'rous tyranny.   265

She gives Saturnius a letter

SATURNINUS *(reads the letter)*

" — and should our plot fail and we miss our mark

(Bassianus 'tis we mean) Sweet Huntsman,

Do the rest and see he goes to his 'reward.'

(You catch our meaning.) Then find yours

Among the nettles 'neath the alder tree   270

Which overhangs the mouth of that same pit

Where we agreed to bury him. Do this,

And we shall be your lasting friends."

O Tamora, was ever heard the like?

This is the pit, and this the alder tree. —   275

Look sirs, if you can find the huntsman out

That was to murder Bassianus here.

AARON

My gracious lord, here is the bag of gold.

SATURNINUS *(to Titus)*

Two of your whelps, these bloody wolverines,

Have here bereft my brother of his life. —   280

Sirs, drag them from the pit unto some cage.

There let them howl until we have devised

Some never-heard-of torture for them both.

TAMORA

What, are they down there? A Miracle! See —

41

How readily the murderers are found!   285

Attendants pull Quintus, Martius,
and the body of Bassianus from the pit

TITUS *(kneeling)*

High Emperor, upon my feeble knee

I beg of you with tears not lightly shed,

Accursèd be my sons if these faults be proved —

But —

SATURNINUS

If it be proved! You see it is apparent.   290

Who found this letter? Tamora, was it you?

TAMORA

Andronicus himself did take it up.

TITUS

I did, my lord, yet let me be their bail,

For by my father's reverend tomb I vow

They shall be ready at your Highness' will   295

To answer these suspicions with their lives.

SATURNINUS

You shall not bail them. See you follow me. —

Some bring the murdered body, some the murderers.

Let them not speak a word. Their guilt is plain.

And, by my soul, were something worse than death,   300

That end upon them should be inflicted.

TAMORA

Andronicus, I'll go entreat the King.

Fear not for your sons; they'll do well enough.

TITUS *(rising)*

Come, Lucius, come. Stay not to talk with them.

They exit, with Attendants leading Martius and Quintus,
and bearing the body of Bassianus

ACT 2 ◆ SCENE 4

Enter the empress' sons, Demetrius and Chiron, with Lavinia, her
hands cut off, and her tongue cut out, and ravished

DEMETRIUS

So, go and tell, and bid thy tongue to speak,

Who 'twas that cut it out and ravished thee.

CHIRON

Mayhap write down thy mind; show thy meaning so,

And if thy stumps will let thee, play the scribe.

DEMETRIUS

See how, even now, she her bloody tokens scrawl!   5

CHIRON *(to Lavinia)*

Go home. For water call; and wash those hands.

DEMETRIUS

She has no tongue to call, nor hands to wash;

And so let's leave her to her silent walks.

CHIRON

Were it my case, I should go hang myself.

DEMETRIUS

If thou had hands to help thee tie the rope.   10

Chiron and Demetrius exit
Enter Marcus from hunting

MARCUS

Who is this? My niece, that flies away so fast?

Cousin, a word! Where is your husband?

If I do dream, I'd give the world to wake.

If I do wake, some planet strike me down

And close these eyes forever 'gainst this sight.   15

Lavinia — it cannot be — Oh, Stay!

Speak, gentle niece. What savage hands

Did make your body bare — and tear and break

Those branches, sweet circling ornaments

43

Where kings have vied to sleep? Some beast! Who? 20
No man would dare — Why dost not speak?
Oh God! Her tongue is cut and where those words
Should be there pours instead a river of her blood —
It rises and it falls between her trembling lips,
And comes and goes with every shuddering breath. 25
No beast but man. Then she is raped by him
And, lest that she accuse him, her tongue cut!
Ah, now you turn'st away your face for shame,
And even as the blood drains from your veins
You blush — shall I speak it for you? 30
Shall I say 'tis so?
Oh that I knew your heart and knew his name
That I might right your wrong and ease my mind,
There was a woman, when they cut her tongue
She stitched the rapist's picture in a sampler. 35
Fair Philomel, who with her needle named Tereus
For his crime. But your Tereus is craftier
And cutting off your fingers stopped your means.
Had the monster ears to hear the music
Your charmed fingers made upon the lute 40
Or the harmony of heaven in your voice —
He would have dropped his knife and prayed to thee.
Come let us go and make thy father blind,
For such a sight will blind a father's eye
Draw not back, for we will mourn with thee. 45
O could our mourning ease thy misery

They exit

ACT 3 ♦ SCENE 1

Enter the Judges and Senators with Titus' two sons (Quintus and Martius) bound, passing on the stage to the place of execution, and Titus going before, pleading

TITUS

Hear me, Grave Fathers; Noble Tribunes, stay.
For pity of mine age, whose youth was spent
In battles' heat while you securely slept;
For all my blood in Rome's great quarrels shed,
For all those freezing nights that I have watched,   5
And for these bitter tears which now you see,
Filling the agèd wrinkles in my cheeks,
Be merciful to my condemnèd sons,
Who never did the deed for which they die.
For two-and-twenty sons I never cried!   10
Because they died in honor's lofty bed.

Andronicus prostrated, and the Judges pass by him.
They exit with the prisoners as Titus continues speaking.

But for these, Tribunes, in the dust I write
My heart's deep anguish with my soul's sad tears.
Let my tears quench the earth's dry appetite
My sons' sweet blood would make it shame and blush.   15
O Earth, I will bequeath thee so much rain
That I'll distil from these two ancient ruins
Than youthful April shall with all his showers.
In summer's drought I'll pelt upon you still;
In winter with warm tears I'll melt the snow   20
And keep eternal springtime on your face,
Will thou refuse to drink my dear sons' blood.

45

Enter Lucius with his weapon drawn

O reverend Tribunes, O gentle agèd men,
Unbind my sons, reverse the doom of death,
Hear me that never wept before, and say   25
My tears may now prevail as orators.

LUCIUS

O noble father, you lament in vain.
The Tribunes hear you not; no man is by,
And you recount your sorrows to the stones.

TITUS

Ah, Lucius, for your brothers let me plead. —   30
Grave tribunes, once more I entreat of you —

LUCIUS

My gracious lord, no tribune hears you speak.

TITUS

Why, 'tis no matter, man. If they did hear,
They would not mark me; if they did mark,
They would not pity me. Yet plead I must,   35
And uselessly, to them.
Therefore I tell my sorrows to the stones,
Who, though they cannot answer my distress,
Yet in some sort are better than the Tribunes,
For that they will not interrupt my grief.   40
When I do weep, they, humbly, at my feet
Receive my tears and seem to weep with me,
And would they only dress in judges' weeds,
Rome could find no tribunes like to these.
A stone is soft as wax, tribunes more hard than the stones;   45
A stone is silent and offendeth not,
And tribunes with their tongues doom men to death.
But wherefore stand'st thou with thy weapon drawn?

LUCIUS

To rescue my two brothers from their death,
For which attempt the Judges have pronounced   50
My everlasting doom of banishment.

TITUS *(rising)*

O happy man, they have protected you!
Why, foolish Lucius, do you not know
That Rome is but a wilderness of tigers?
Tigers must prey, and Rome no other prey   55
Than me and mine. How happy are you then
To banished be from those who'd feed on ye —
But who comes with our brother Marcus here?

Enter Marcus with Lavinia

MARCUS

Titus, prepare your agèd eyes to weep,
Or, if not so, your noble heart to break.   60
I bring consuming sorrow to your age.

TITUS

Can it consume me? Then bring it on me, then.

MARCUS

This was your daughter.

TITUS

Why, Marcus, so she is.

LUCIUS *(falling to his knees)*

Ay me, this object kills me!   65

TITUS

Faint-hearted boy, arise and look upon her. —
Speak, Lavinia. What accursèd hand
Hath made thee handless in thy father's sight?
What fool hath added water to the sea
Or brought a flaming torch to burning Troy?   70

LUCIUS

    Speak, gentle sister. Who hath martyred thee?

MARCUS

    That sweet melodious bird that sang her thought,

    Enchanting every ear with pleasing eloquence,

    Is torn by force from forth its hollow cage

    And can no more sing its sweet and varied notes   75

    Enchanting every ear —

LUCIUS

    Then speak you for her, who hath done this thing!

MARCUS

    Thus I found her straying in the park,

    Seeking to hide herself as doth the deer

    That has received a wound past curing.   80

TITUS

    It was my Dear, and he that wounded her

    Has hurt me more than had he killed me dead.

    Oh, had I but seen thy picture in this plight

    It would have made me mad. What shall I do

    Now I behold your lovely body so?   85

    Thou has not hands to wipe away thy tears,

    Nor tongue to tell who has martyred thee.

    Thy husband he is dead, and for his death

    Thy brothers are condemned and dead by this —

    Look, Marcus! — Ah, son Lucius, look on her!   90

    When I did name her brothers, then fresh tears

    Stood on her cheeks as weeping drops upon

    a severed lily almost withered —

MARCUS

    She would weep had they killed her husband —

    She would weep did she know them innocent —   95

TITUS

    If they did kill thy husband, then be glad,

    For then the law hath ta'en revenge on them. —

    No, no, they would not do so foul a deed.

    Witness the sorrow that their sister makes. —

    Gentle Lavinia, come let me kiss thee,   100

    Or make some other sign what I may do.

    Shall we four, like broken figures at a fountain,

    Sit round and downward gaze to see our cheeks,

    How they are stained like meadows yet not dry

    With miry slime left on them by a flood?   105

    And in the fountain shall we weep so long

    Till the fresh taste be taken from that clearness

    And we have made a brine pit with our bitter tears?

    Or shall we cut away our hands like thine?

    Or shall we bite off our tongues and in dumb shows   110

    In soundless frenzies pass our hateful days?

    What shall we do? Let us that still can speak

    Devise some plot of such inspired misery

    We shall still be gaped upon in time to come.

LUCIUS

    Sweet father, cease your tears, for at your grief   115

    See how my wretched sister sobs and weeps.

MARCUS

    Patience, dear niece — Good Titus, dry your eyes.

TITUS

    Ah Marcus, Marcus, Brother, well I know

    Your handkerchief is full and cannot hold my tears,

    For you, poor man, hast drowned it with your own.   120

LUCIUS

    Ah, my Lavinia, I will wipe thy cheeks.

TITUS

Mark, Marcus, Mark. I understand her signs.
Had she a tongue to speak, now would she say
That to her brother which I said to you.
His handkerchief so overwet with woe   125
Can do no service on her flooding cheeks.
O, what an symphony of woe is this,
As far from help as hell from bliss!

Enter Aaron the Moor alone

AARON

Titus Andronicus, my lord the Emperor
Sends you this word, that if thou love your sons,   130
Let Marcus, Lucius, or yourself, old Titus,
Or any one of you chop off your hand
And send it to the King; and he for that
Will send you hither both your sons alive
And that shall be the ransom for their fault.   135

TITUS

O gracious emperor! O gentle Aaron!
Did ever raven sing so like a lark,
That gives sweet tidings of the rising sun?
With all my heart I'll send the Emperor my hand.
Good Aaron, you will chop it off yourself!   140

LUCIUS

Stay, father, for that brave hand of yours,
That hath thrown down so many enemies,
Shall not be chopped. My hand will serve the turn.
My youth can better spare my blood than you,
And therefore mine shall save my brothers' lives.   145

MARCUS

Which of your hands have not defended Rome
And have reared aloft the bloody battle ax,

Scrawling red destruction on enemy's walls?
My hand has been idle, let it now serve
To ransom my two nephews from their death.   150
Then have I sent it to a worthy end.

AARON

Nay, come, agree whose hand shall serve the turn
For fear all die before their pardon come.

MARCUS

My hand shall go.

LUCIUS

By heaven, it shall not go!   155

TITUS

Agree between you. I will spare my hand.

LUCIUS

Then I'll go fetch an ax.

MARCUS

But I will use the ax.

Lucius and Marcus exit

TITUS

Come hither, Aaron, I'll deceive them both.
Lend me your hand, and I will give you mine.   160

AARON *(aside)*

If this be called "deceit" — I'll give it up
And never while I live deceive men more.
But hmm, and no, I fear that may not last.
And that you'll see ere half an hour pass.

He cuts off Titus' hand
Enter Lucius and Marcius again

TITUS

Now stay your strife. What shall be is done —   165
Good Aaron, give his Majesty my hand.
Tell him it was a hand that kept him

From a thousand dangers. Bid him bury it.
More it hath merited; but that much at least.
As for my sons, say I account of them   170
As jewels purchased at an easy price,
And yet dear, too, for I bought back mine own.

AARON

I go, Andronicus, and for your hand
Look soon to see the faces of your boys.

(aside)

Though all the rest go missing. O, how evil —   175
Feeds me with the very thought of it!
Leave good for fools and to the Pallid, grace;
Aaron would have his soul black like his face.

Aaron exits

TITUS

O, here I lift this one hand up to heaven,
And bow this feeble ruin to the earth.   180

(he kneels)

If any power pities wretches' tears,
To that I call.

(Lavinia kneels)

What, wouldst thou kneel with me?
Do, then, dear heart, for heaven shall hear our prayers,
Or with our sighs we'll breathe the brightness dim —   185
And stain the sun with fog, as sometime clouds
When they do hug him in their melting bosoms.

MARCUS

Oh, brother, tether your speech to what is,
And do not break into these deep extremes.

TITUS

Is not my sorrow deep, having no bottom?   190
Then how should I limit my lament?

52

MARCUS

But yet let reason govern your lament.

TITUS

If there were reason for these miseries,
Then in bundles I could bind my woes.
When skies weep, doth not the Earth o'erflow?   195
If the winds rage, doth not the sea wax mad,
Threat'ning the heavens with his big-swoll'n face?
And will you have a reason for convulsion?
I am the sea. Hark how her sighs doth flow!
She is weeping heaven, I am the Earth.   200
Then must my sea be moved with her sighs;
Then must my Earth with her continual tears
Become a deluge, overflowed and drowned,
And so my bowels cannot conceal those woes
But like a drunkard must I vomit them.   205
Then give me leave, for losers will have leave
To ease their stomachs with their bitter heaving.

Enter a Messenger with two heads and a hand

MARCUS

Here's a riddle worse than ever Sphinx devised
What man is, has one head, yet bears two
Two hands he has yet bears another one —   210

MESSENGER

Worthy Andronicus, ill you are repaid
For that good hand you sent the Emperor.
Here are the heads of your two noble sons,
And here's that hand in scorn sent back to you.
Your grief their sport, your offering mocked,   215
And so more woe to me to think on thee
Than on the death of my own father.

He exits

MARCUS

Now let hot Etna cool in Sicily,

And be my heart an everflowing hell!

These miseries are more than may be borne.   220

To weep with those that weep some peace provides,

But to mock their sorrow is to slay them twice.

LUCIUS

Ah, that this sight should make so deep a wound

And yet detested life not drain away!

That death should let life bear his name,   225

Where life hath scarce the motion left to breathe.

Lavinia kisses Titus

MARCUS,

Alas, poor heart, that kiss is comfortless

As frozen water to a shriveled snake.

TITUS

When will this fearful slumber have an end?

MARCUS

I will not lie to you. Die, Andronicus.   230

You do not slumber. There your two sons' heads,

Your warlike hand, your mangled daughter here,

Your other banish'd son by this dear sight

Struck pale and bloodless; here your brother, I,

Even like a stony image, cold and numb.   235

No more will I advise you check your griefs.

Rend your silver hair, tear your other hand,

Gnaw it with your teeth, and be this dismal sight

The closing up of our most wretched eyes.

Now is a time to storm. Why art thou still?   240

TITUS

Ha, ha, ha!

54

MARCUS

    Why do you laugh? It fits not with this hour.

          Titus and Lavinia rise

TITUS

    Well. I have not another tear to shed.

    Besides, this sorrow is an enemy

    That would invade my watering eyes   245

    And blind them with obligatory tears.

    And then how shall I find Revenge's cave?

    These fragments of my children seem to speak

    And whisper I shall never come to bliss

    Till all these evils be returned again   250

    Even down the throats of those that smite us.

    Come, let me see what task I have to do.

    You wretched people, circle me about

    That I may turn me to each one of you

    And swear unto my soul to right your wrongs.   255

    The vow is made. Come brother, catch! A head,

    And with one hand its brother will I bear. —

    And, Lavinia, now take thy Father's hand,

    (Not that one, this one, wench, between thy teeth)

    As for thee, boy, go get thee from my sight.   260

    Thou art an exile, and thou must not stay.

    Hie to the Goths and raise an army there.

    And if you love me, as I think you do,

    Let's kiss and part, for we have much to do.

          All but Lucius exit

LUCIUS

    Farewell, Andronicus, my noble father,   265

    The woefullest of men that ever lived

    Farewell, cold Rome, till Lucius come again.

    You hold those hostage dearer than my life.

Farewell, Lavinia, my noble sister.
I would we were as once we were but that —   270
Is done, and we live in Oblivion
And a land of everlasting grief.
But as I live I will revenge your wrongs.
And make proud Saturnine and his empress
Beg the gates like Tarquin and his queen.   275
Now will I to the Goths and raise a power
To be revenged on Rome and Saturnine.

Lucius Exits

INTERMISSION

ACT 3 ◆ SCENE 2

A BANQUET

Enter Titus Andronicus, Marcus, Lavinia,
and the boy, Young Lucius, with Servants

TITUS

So, so. Now sit, and look you eat no more
Than will just preserve in us such strength
As will revenge our bitter woes. Marcus —
Unknit your arms — that sorrow-wreathen knot.
Your niece and I, poor creatures, want our hands   5
And cannot passionate our tenfold grief
With folded arms. This poor right hand of mine
Is left to tyrannize upon my breast,
Who when my heart, all mad with misery,
Beats in this hollow prison of my flesh,   10
Then thus I thump it down. —

(to Lavinia)

Thou map of wounds, that thus must talk by signs,
While thy poor heart is hurtling 'gainst its bars,
Thou canst not strike it thus — to make it still.

56

Then wound it with sighing, girl, kill it with groans; 15
Or get some little knife between thy teeth
And just against thy heart make thou a hole,
That all the tears that thy poor eyes let fall
May run into the drain and, soaking in,
Drown the lamenting fool in sea-salt tears. 20

MARCUS

Fie, brother, fie! Teach her not thus to lay
Such violent hands upon her tender life.

TITUS

How now! Has sorrow made thee dull?
Why no man can be mad here but myself!
What violent hands can she lay on her life? 25
The very word of "hands" to one "be-handed" —
Is to bid Aeneas tell the tale twice o'er
How Troy was burnt and he made miserable!
'Tis a touch-y subject, to talk of hands,
Lest we do remember that we two have none. — 30
On the other hand, how frantically I talk,
As if we could forget we had no hands
If Marcus did not name the word of "hand"!
Come, let's fall to, and, gentle girl, eat this.
Give her no drink! — Hark, Marcus, what she says. 35
I can interpret all her martyred signs.
She says she drinks no other drink but tears
Brewed with her sorrow, mashed upon her cheeks. —
Speechless complainer, I will learn thy thought.
In thy dumb action will I be as perfect 40
As begging hermits in their holy prayers.
Thou shall not sigh, nor hold thy stumps to heaven,
Nor wink, nor nod, nor kneel, nor make a sign,
But I of these will wrest an alphabet

And by still practice learn to know thy meaning. 45

YOUNG LUCIUS *(weeping)*

Good grandsire, leave these bitter deep laments.

Make my aunt merry with some pleasing tale.

MARCUS

Alas, the tender boy, in passion moved,

Doth weep to see his grandsire's heaviness.

TITUS

Peace, tender sapling. Thou art made of tears, 50

And tears will quickly melt thy life away.

(Marcus strikes the dish with a knife)

What dost thou strike at, Marcus, with thy knife?

MARCUS

At that I have killed, my lord, a fly.

TITUS

Out on thee, murderer! Thou kill'st my heart.

Mine eyes are gorged and sick on tyranny; 55

This deed of death done on the innocent

Becomes not Titus' brother. Get thee gone.

I see thou art not for my company.

MARCUS

Alas, my lord, I have but killed a fly.

TITUS

"But"? How if that fly had a father and mother? 60

How would he hang his slender gilded wings

And buzz, lamenting doings in the air!

Poor harmless fly,

That, with his pretty buzzing melody,

Came here to make us merry! And thou hast killed him. 65

MARCUS

Pardon me, sir. It was a dark, ill-favored fly,

Like to the Empress' Moor. Therefore I killed him.

TITUS

    O, O, O,

    O, there's a horse of other color,

    Then pardon me for censuring thee.   70

    Give me thy knife, and I will kill him more

    Flattering myself as if he were the Moor

    Come hither purposely to poison me.

    There's for thyself, and that's for Tamora.

    Ah, sirrah!   75

    See, I think we are not brought so low

    But that between us we cannot kill a fly

    That comes in likeness of a coal-black Moor.

MARCUS

    Alas, poor man, grief has so unmade him

    He takes false shadows for true substance.   80

TITUS

    Come, away. — Lavinia, go with me.

    We'll to thy chamber and I'll read to thee

    Sad stories told since the times of old. —

    Come, boy, and come with us. Thine eyes are young,

    And thou shalt read when mine begin to fill.   85

They exit

ACT 4 ◆ SCENE 1

Enter Lucius' son and Lavinia running after him
The boy flies from her with his books under his arm
Enter Titus and Marcus

YOUNG LUCIUS

Help, grandsire, help! My aunt Lavinia
Follows me everywhere, I know not why. —
Good uncle Marcus, see how she pursues me! —
Alas, sweet aunt, I know not what you mean.

MARCUS

Stand by me Lucius. Do not fear your aunt.   5

TITUS

She cares for you, boy, too well to do thee harm.

YOUNG LUCIUS

Ay, when my father was yet at home she did.

MARCUS

What means my niece Lavinia by these signs!

TITUS

Fear her not, Lucius, there's something that she wants.

MARCUS

There's somewhere she would have you go with her.   10
Ah, boy, a mother never with more care
Read to a son than she hath read to you
Cicero, and Ovid, and sweet poetry
You know no reason why she so pursues you?

YOUNG LUCIUS

My lord, I know none, I, nor can I guess,   15
Unless some fit or madness do possess her;
(For often I have heard my grandsire say,

Extremity of grief makes men run mad,
And I had read that Hecuba of Troy
Ran mad for sorrow. That made me fear 20
Even though I know my noble aunt
Loves me as my mother, when she ran at me,
And she did in this frenzy fright me so
I, startled, clutched my books and did her fly
Thoughtlessly, I own. — Oh pardon me, sweet aunt. 25
And madam (if my Uncle Marcus go)
I will most willingly attend your ladyship.

MARCUS

Lucius, I will.

TITUS

How now, Lavinia! — Marcus what means this?
It is his book there that she gestures at. 30
Which is it, girl, of these? Open them, boy. —

(to Lavinia)

But you art far the deeper reader.
Come and take choice of all my library,
And so beguile thy sorrow till the heavens
Reveal that cursed man that did this deed. 35
Why lifts she up her arms thus — one then two?

MARCUS

I think she means that there were more than one
Confederate in the fact. Ay, more there was,
Or she lifts them up to heaven for revenge.

TITUS

Lucius, what is that book she strikes at? 40

YOUNG LUCIUS

Grandsire, 'tis Ovid's Metamorphosis.
My mother gave it me —

MARCUS

   — For love of her,

   Perhaps, she culled it from among the rest.

TITUS

   Soft! How frantically she mauls the pages.   45

   Help her!

   What does she find? — Lavinia, shall I read?

   Here the tragic tale of Philomel,

   It speaks of Tereus' treason and his rape.

   And rape, I fear, the root of thy assault.   50

MARCUS

   See! How she thumps her stumps upon the page!

TITUS

   Lavinia, wert savaged so, sweet girl,

   Ravished and hurt as Philomela was,

   Forced in the ruthless, vast and gloomy woods?

   And pictured here — a place as where we hunted! —   55

   O, had we never never hunted there! —

   Patterned by the poet, here described —

   "By nature made for murders and for rapes."

MARCUS

   O, why should nature build so foul a den,

   Unless the gods delight in tragedies?   60

TITUS

   Give signs, sweet girl, for here are none but friends,

   What Roman lord it was durst do the deed.

   Or was it Saturnine himself, as Tarquin once,

   That left the camp to sin in Lucrece's bed?

MARCUS

   Sit down, sweet niece, Brother, sit by me.   65

(they sit)

   Apollo, Pallas, Mercury inspire us —

How we may this treason find — By Jove!
Write their names, Girl, that we may right your wrongs
(he writes his name with his staff, and guides it with feet and mouth)
This sandy plot our page; do, if you can,
What I have done. I have writ my name   70
Without the help of any hand at all.
(she takes the staff in her mouth and guides it with her stumps
and writes)
Accurs'd be they that forced us to this shift!
Write down, good niece, and here unearth at last
What God for justice wishes to reveal.
Heaven guide thy pen to print your sorrow clear,   75
That we may know the traitors and the truth.
TITUS
O, do you read, my lord, what she has writ?
MARCUS
Stuprum — !
TITUS
O — O Raped and broken! Chiron and Demetrius.
MARCUS
What, what! The lustful sons of Tamora   80
Performed this bloody, hideous, deed?
TITUS
God in Heaven! Why are you deaf and blind!
MARCUS
O, Brother, if you can, be calm although
There is that written on this sandy page
To stir a mutiny in the gentlest men —   85
And arm the minds of infants to rebel.
My lord, kneel down with me. — Lavinia, kneel. —
And kneel, sweet boy, your noble father's hope,
(they all kneel)

And swear with me as did Lucretia's father
Swear revenge for fair Lucrece's rape —   90
We shall avenge this blameless ruined girl,
And clear in mind and cold of blood will wreak
Mortal havoc on these traitorous Goths,
And see their blood or die in the attempt.

They rise

TITUS

'Tis sure enough, if only you knew how.   95
But if you hunt these wolf cubs, then beware;
Their dam will catch your scent and wake at once.
She's with the lion deeply still in bed,
And lulls him whilst she plays him on her back;
While he lies sleeping, she will be doing.   100
You are a young huntsman, Marcus; this is for me.
And I will go and get a plate of brass,
And with a steel point there engrave her words,
And keep them safe. The angry northern wind
Will sands erase and so our daughter's scrawls   105
And where's our lesson then? — Boy, what say you?

YOUNG LUCIUS

I say, my lord, that if I were a man,
E'en their mother's bedchamber could not
Keep safe these vile hostages of Rome!

MARCUS

Ay, that's my boy! Your father hath full oft   110
For his ungrateful country done the like.

YOUNG LUCIUS

And, uncle, so will I and if I live.

TITUS

Come, go with me into mine armory.
Lucius, and I'll fit thee like a knight and then

Shalt carry from me to the Empress' sons   115
Fine Presents I intend to send them both.

Come. You'll give my message, boy, will you?

YOUNG LUCIUS

Ay, with my dagger in their bosoms, grandsire.

TITUS

No, boy, not so. We'll take another course. —
Lavinia, come. — Marcus, look to my house.   120
Lucius and I'll go show ourselves at court;
Ay, marry will we, sir, and we'll be waited on.

All but Marcus exit

MARCUS

Oh, heavens, can you see a mind so stricken
And not relent, nor have compassion on him?
Marcus care for him in his madness,   125
He has more scars of sorrow in his heart
Than Enemies' marks upon his battered shield,
But yet so just he will not take revenge
Revenge him, heavens, and be then his arm.

He exits

ACT 4 ◆ SCENE 2

Enter Aaron, Chiron, and Demetrius at one door,
and at the other door, young Lucius and another,
with a bundle of weapons and verses written upon them

CHIRON

Demetrius, here's the son of Lucius.

He has some message to deliver us.

AARON

Ay, some mad message from his mad granddad.

YOUNG LUCIUS

My lords, with all the humbleness I may

I greet your Honors from Andronicus —   5
(aside)

And pray the Roman Gods destroy you both.
DEMETRIUS

Gramercy, Luscious Lucius. What's the news?
YOUNG LUCIUS *(aside)*

That you are both revealed, that's the news,
For villains marked with rape. — May it please you,
My Grandsire, in his wisdom, has sent by me   10
The very best weapons of his armory
To glorify your honorable youth,
The hope of Rome; for so he bid me say,
And so I do, and give these gifts to you
Your Lordships, so that should the need arise,   15
You may be both armed and armored well,
And so I leave you both
(aside)

— like bloody villains.

He exits, with Attendant

DEMETRIUS

What's here? A scroll, and written round about.
Let's see: 20
(he reads)

"*Integer vitae, scerique purus, Non eget Mauri Iaculis, nec arcu.*" Why this is Greek to me —
CHIRON

'Tis Latin, Fool, a verse in Horace: And I know it well.
I read it in my Grammar long ago.
An upright man needs not a Moor —   25
To defend him — (whatever THAT means …)
AARON

Ay, just. A verse in Horace; right, you have it.

(aside)

So speaks the asses' brother! What things they are.
This is no jest. The old man knows their guilt
And sends them weapons wrapped about with lines   30
That would wound (were they not halfwits) to the core.
Were our witty empress not brought a-bed,
She would get the gist and admire the jest.
But let her rest as best she can for now —
And now, young lords, was't not a lucky star   35
Brought us here to Rome, Strangers, or worse —
Captives, to be advancèd to this height?
It did me good before the palace gate
To mock the Tribune in his brother's hearing.

DEMETRIUS

But me more good to see so great a lord   40
Basely to bow and scrape and send us gifts.

AARON

Had he not reason to be friendly, my Lord?
Did you not use his daughter very friendly?

DEMETRIUS

I would we had a thousand Roman Ladies
To be such friends, by turns, to serve our lust.   45

CHIRON

A charitable wish and full of love!

AARON

Not without your Mother gives her blessing.

CHIRON

And that would she, and wish us twenty thousand more.

DEMETRIUS

Come, Let us go and pray to all the gods
For our beloved mother in her pains.   50

AARON *(aside)*

    Pray to the devils; the gods have given us over.

               Trumpets sound offstage

DEMETRIUS

    Why trumpet the trumpets?

CHIRON

    It must mean the Emperor has a son —

DEMETRIUS

    Soft, who comes here?

          Enter Nurse with Moorish child in her arms

NURSE

    Good morrow, lords.   55

    O, tell me, did you see Aaron the Moor?

AARON

    Well, more or less, or ne'er a whit at all,

    Here Aaron is. And what with Aaron now?

NURSE

    O gentle Aaron, we are all undone!

    Now help or woe betide us evermore.   60

AARON

    Why, what a caterwauling do you keep!

    What do you wrap and fumble in your arms?

NURSE

    Oh, that which I would hide from heaven's eye,

    Our Empress' shame and stately Rome's disgrace.

    She is delivered, lords, she is delivered.   65

AARON

    To whom?

NURSE

    Of what, you mean. She is brought a-bed.

AARON

    Well, God give her good rest. What has he sent her?

NURSE

A devil.

AARON

Well, she is the devil's dam. A proper issue!   70

NURSE

A joyless, dismal, black, and sorrowful issue!

Here is the babe, as loathsome as a toad

To all the pale-faced breeders of our clime.

The Empress sends it thee, thy stamp, thy seal,

And bids thee christen it with thy dagger's point.   75

AARON

Zounds, you whore, is black so base a hue?

(to the baby)

Sweet bud, you are a beauteous blossom, sure.

DEMETRIUS

Villain, what has thou done?

AARON

That which you canst not undo.

CHIRON

You have undone our mother.   80

AARON

Actually, I have done your mother.

DEMETRIUS

And by that, hell dog, she is undone.

Dead her chances are, due to you! Her loathed choice!

Accursed the offspring of so foul a fiend!

CHIRON

It shall not live.   85

AARON

It shall not die.

NURSE

Aaron, it must. Its mother wills it so.

AARON

    What, must it, nurse? Then let no man but I

    Do execution on my flesh and blood.

DEMETRIUS

    I'll skewer the tadpole on my rapier's point.   90

    Nurse give it me. My sword shall soon dispatch it.

AARON (taking the baby)

    Sooner will this sword plow up thy bowels!

    Stay, murderous villains, will kill your brother?

    Now, by the burning tapers of the sky

    That shone so bright the night this boy was got,   95

    You die upon my scimitar's sharp point

    That touches this my firstborn son and heir.

    I tell you, imp-lings, not Enceladus —

    Nor great Alcides — Oh never mind —

    Sufficeth it to say —   100

    You shall not seize your prey out of his father's hands.

    Come, Come, you bloody shallow-hearted boys!

    You white-washed walls, you alehouse painted signs!

    My coal-black is purer than your hue

    For coal-black scorns to bear another hue;   105

    And all the water in the ocean

    Can never turn the swan's black legs to white,

    Although she wash them hourly in the flood.

    Tell the Empress from me I'm old enough

    To keep mine own, explain it how she may.   110

DEMETRIUS

    Will you betray your noble mistress so?

AARON

    My mistress is — a mistress. But he a little me.

    The vigor and the picture of my youth.

    And before the world I do prefer him:

And he — despite of you — I will keep safe.   115
Or some of you shall smoke for it in Rome.

DEMETRIUS

By this our mother is forever shamed.

CHIRON

Rome will despise her for this foul escape.

NURSE

The Emperor in his rage will doom her death.

CHIRON

I blush to think upon the shame.   120

AARON

Why, there's the liability your privilege bears —
That treacherous hue betrays with blushing
The secrets and close counsels of thy hearts.
Now here's a fellow cut of other cloth.
Look how the little scamp beams on his father,   125
As if to say, "Old lad, I am thine own!"
And he is your brother, lords, fed
Of self-same blood that first gave life to you,
And from that womb where you two first were penned
He also quickened and grew to the light.   130
Nay, mothers are known, fathers less than sure.
(But he is me in miniature.)

NURSE

Aaron, what shall I say unto the Empress?

DEMETRIUS

Tell us, Aaron, what is to be done,
And we will all submit to thy advice   135
Save the child, then, if we may all be safe.

AARON

Now sit where I can see you and consult.
My son and I will take the downwind side —

Beware. Now. Now let us talk of your safety.

DEMETRIUS *(to the nurse)*

How many women saw this child of his? 140

AARON

That's the spirit! Put heads together then

I'm a lamb; but if you challenge the Moor,

The cornered boar, the mountain lioness,

The ocean rages not so much as Aaron storms.

(to the nurse)

But say again. How many saw the child? 145

NURSE

Cornelia the midwife, and myself,

And no one else but the delivered Empress.

AARON

The Empress, the midwife, and yourself.

Two may keep counsel when the third's away.

Go to the Empress; tell her I said this. 150

(he kills her)

"This little piggy cried Wheak, Wheak, Wheak"

All the way to the spit.

DEMETRIUS

What mean'st you Aaron? Why did you that?

AARON

Oh Lord sir, 'tis a necessary thing.

Shall she live to betray this guilt of ours, 155

A long-tongued babbling gossip? No, lord, no.

And now be it known to you my full intent;

Not far, lives one Muliteus, my countryman

Whose lady yesternight was brought to bed.

She is white, his child is like to her. 160

Go plot with him and give the mother gold,

And tell them both the circumstance of all,

And how by this their child shall be advanced,
And be receivèd for the emperor's heir,
And substituted in the place of mine   165
To calm this tempest whirling in the court,
And let the emperor dandle him for his own.
Hark ye, I gave our nurse the coup de grâce
And you must needs conduct the funeral;
The field is near and you are gallant grooms.   170
This done, see that you take no naps
But send the midwife presently to me.
The midwife and the nurse well made away,
Then let the ladies babble what they may.

CHIRON

Aaron, I see you will not trust the air   175
With secrets.

DEMETRIUS

For this care of Tamora
Herself and hers are highly bound to you.

Exit Chiron and Demetrius with dead Nurse

AARON

Now to the Goths as swift as swallows fly,
There to dispose this treasure in mine arms   180
And secretly to greet the empress' friends
And they will bear you to those will keep you.
Come my full-lipped blossom, there is work to do —
For it is you that puts us to our trouble
Oh, I'll have you fed on berries and on roots,   185
And feed on curds and whey, and suck the goat,
And cabin in a cave and by this bringing up
You'll be a warrior and command a camp.
Smile at me thou imp?

He exits with the baby

ACT 4 ◆ SCENE 3

Enter Titus, old Marcus, his son Publius, young Lucius,
and other gentlemen (Caius and Sempronius) with bows
and Titus bears the arrows with letters on the ends of them

TITUS

Come Marcus, come. Kinsmen, this is the way. —
Sir boy, let me see your archery.
Draw back farther yet and 'tis there straight! —
"*Terras Astraea reliquit*." "See how Justice Flies!"
Remember it, Marcus, she's gone, she's fled. —   5
Sirs, take you to your tools. You, cousins, shall
Go sound the ocean and cast your nets;
Happily you may catch Justice in the sea;
Yet there's as little justice there as land.
No; Publius and Sempronius, you must do it.   10
'Tis you must dig with pickax and with spade,
And pierce the inmost center of the Earth.
Then, when you come to Pluto's region,
I pray you, deliver him this petition.
Tell him it is for justice and for aid,   15
And that it comes from old Andronicus,
Shaken with sorrows in ungrateful Rome.
Ah, Rome! Well, Well, I did make thee miserable
As I did throw the people under him,
Saturninus, that does tyrannize o'er me.   20
Go, get you gone, and pray be careful all,
And leave you not a man-of-war unsearched.
For Justice for he may have shipped her hence,
Then, Kinsmen, we may whistle in the wind for her.

MARCUS

O Publius, is it not too much to bear   25
To see thy noble uncle so unmoored?

75

PUBLIUS

    Therefore, friends, leave him not alone

    By day and night attend his every move,

    And humor him as gently as you may

    And pray that time provide some remedy —   30

MARCUS

    Kinsmen, his sorrows are past remedy

    But fury in its stead begins to flow —

    We'll join the Goths and in revengeful war

    We'll havoc wreak on Rome for its ingratitude

    And vengeance take on traitor Saturnine.   35

TITUS

    Publius, how now? How now, my masters?

    What, have you met with Justice?

PUBLIUS

    No, my good lord, but Pluto sends you word,

    If you will pluck Revenge from hell, you shall.

    But, alas, for Justice, she's so very busy   40

    (He thinks, perhaps with Jove above, or elsewhere,)

    That you might need to wait some while for her.

TITUS

    He does me wrong to feed me with delays.

    I'll plunge into the burning lake myself

    And pull her out of Hades by the heels!   45

    Marcus, we are no shrubs or saplings we,

    Nor big boned giants framed to Cyclops' size,

    But metal, Marcus, steel to the very back,

    Yet wrung with wrongs more than our backs can bear;

    And since there's no Justice in Earth nor Hell,   50

    We will beseech Heaven and move the gods

    To send down Justice to right our wrongs.

    Come to our doing. You are a good archer, Marcus.

He gives them arrows

Here's to Jove, that's for you: Here to Apollo,
To Mars, that's for myself, here, boy, to Athena,   55
Here to Mercury, to Saturn, Caius — not to Saturnine!
You were as well to shoot against the wind.
To it, boy! — Marcus, let fly when I bid.
On my word, I have written to effect;
There's not a god left unsolicited.   60

MARCUS

Kinsmen, shoot all your shafts into the court.
We will afflict the Emperor in his pride.

TITUS

Now, masters, draw.

(they shoot)

O, well aimed, Lucius!
Ha, ha!   65
Publius, Publius, what have you done?
See, see, you have shot off one of Taurus' horns!

MARCUS

My lord; when Publius shot,
The Bull, being galled, gave Aries such a knock
That down fell both the Ram's horns in the court,   70
And who should find them but the Empress' Toy?
She laughed and told the Moor he must needs
Go hang them on his master for a cuckold.

TITUS

Why, there's the ticket! God give his Lordship joy!
Enter a country fellow with a basket and two pigeons in it
News dropped from the sky! See, the postman's come.   75
Sirrah, what tidings? Have you any letters?
Shall I have Justice, What says Jupiter?

77

COUNTRY FELLOW

    Ho, thet feller builds the gallows? He sayeth

    He took 'em down again, for the man must

    Not be hanged till the next week.   80

TITUS

    But what says Jupiter, I ask thee?

COUNTRY FELLOW

    Alas, sir, I know not Jubiter; I never

    Drank with such a feller of that name.

TITUS

    Why, varlet, art thou not the carrier?

COUNTRY FELLOW

    Ay, of my pigeons, sir; nothing else.   85

TITUS

    Why, didst thou not just come from heaven?

COUNTRY FELLOW

    From heaven? Alas, sir, I never came from there. God forbid I

    should be so bold as to go to heaven while so youthful. No,

    I be going with my pigeons to the people's court, to argument

    an matter of brawl betwixt my uncle and one of the Emper-   90

    or's men.

MARCUS *(to Titus)*

    Why, sir, here's a perfect vessel for your brief; let him deliver

    the pigeons to the Emperor from you.

TITUS

    Tell me, can you deliver a petition to the Emperor with grace?

COUNTRY FELLOW

    Nay, truly sir, I could never say grace in all my life.   95

TITUS

    Never mind, come hither. Make no more ado,

    But give your pigeons to the Emperor.

    I promise you'll have justice at his hands.

Hold, hold; meanwhile here's money for your
Pains — Give me pen and ink. — Sirrah, can you   100
Supplicate? Deliver up a supplication?

He writes

COUNTRY FELLOW

I can try, sir. How?

TITUS

Here is the supplication. When you see him, at first approach
you kneel, then kiss his foot, then deliver your pigeons, then
look for your reward. I'll be watching. See you do it bravely.   105

He hands him a scroll

COUNTRY FELLOW

Upon my word, Sir. Let me go at it.

TITUS

Sirrah, hast thou a knife? Come let me see it. —

(he takes the knife and gives it to Marcus)

Here, Marcus, conceal it in this paper,
Made to look as humble as the bearer —
And when you have given it to the Emperor,   110
Come and tell me what it is he says.

COUNTRY FELLOW

God be with you, sir. I surely will.

He exits

TITUS

Come Marcus, let us go. — Publius, follow us.

They exit

ACT 4 ◆ SCENE 4

Enter Emperor Saturninus, and Empress Tamora and her two sons,
Chiron and Demetrius, with Attendants. The Emperor brings the
arrows in his hand that Titus shot at him.

SATURNINUS

Why, lords, what wrongs are these! Has ever been
An emperor in Rome upbraided so,
Tormented, confronted with such contempt
All for wielding even-handed justice?
My lords, you well know, as know well the gods,   5
Whatever these disturbers of the peace
Do buzz in people's ears, we've nothing done
But what is law against those wicked sons
Of old Andronicus. So what and if
His sorrows have so overwhelmed his wits?   10
Shall we then be affronted in his madness,
His fits, his frenzy, and his bitterness?
And now he writes to be put right by heaven!
See, here's "to Jove," and this "to Mercury,"
This "to Apollo" this to the god of war.   15
Oh, nice scrolls to fly about the streets of Rome!
What's this but libel against the Senate
And to broadly cast of my injustice?
A goodly gambit is it not, my lords?
That he should say, in Rome no Justice lives.   20
But as I live, his put-on madness
Shall be no hiding for these outrages,
And he and his shall find that justice lives
In Saturninus' stealth — if they dare sleep
They'll be awaked by such a fury shall   25
Cut off the proud'st conspirator that lives.

TAMORA

My gracious lord, my lovely Saturnine,

Lord of my life, commander of my thoughts,

Calm yourself, and bear in mind poor Titus' years,   30

His weight of sorrow for those valiant sons,

Whose loss has pierced him deep and scarred his heart,

And comfort him instead in his distress

Before you persecute the least or best

For this contempt they raise on his behalf.   35

(aside)

(Why, then it's Mother's turn again — Quick, Wits!

Little I must play all sides at once.

But, Titus, I did wound you to the core.

Your lifeblood's gone. If Aaron now be wise,

Then we are safe, the anchor dropped in port.)   40

Enter Country Fellow

How now, good fellow, would you speak with us?

COUNTRY FELLOW

Yea, forsooth, and your Mistressship be the emperial.

TAMORA

"Empress" I am, Dear Rustic, there the "Emperor."

COUNTRY FELLOW

'Tis he! — God and Saint Stephen give you good e'en. I have

brought you a letter and a couple of pigeons here.   45

Saturninus reads the letter

SATURNINUS

Go, take him away and hang him. NOW!

COUNTRY FELLOW

Oh, Thank ye your majesty. And how much will ye pay me?

TAMORA

Come Sirrah, you must be hanged.

COUNTRY FELLOW

Hanged! Well I'll be danged.

He exits with Attendants

SATURNINUS

Despiteful and intolerable wrongs!   50

Shall I endure this monstrous villainy?

Again these accusations come and more!

Must this be borne? He claims his traitorous sons

That died by law for murder of our brother,

Have by my means been butchered wrongfully!   55

Go, drag Andronicus hither by the hair.

Neither age nor honor shall protect him.

For this abuse, I'll slaughter him myself

Sly, frantic wretch, that helped to make me great

Only so that he should govern Rome and me.   60

Enter Aemilius

What news with you, Aemilius?

AEMILIUS

To Arms, my lords! Rome never had more cause.

The Goths have gathered and with a power

Of deadly men they come, hell-bent on ruin,

They march towards us under the command   65

Of Lucius, son to old Andronicus,

Who threatens in pursuit of his revenge,

To do us worse than Coriolanus did.

SATURNINUS

Is warlike Lucius general of the Goths?

These tidings hit me most where I do live —   70

As flowers with frost or grass beat down with storms.

Ay, now begins our sorrows to approach.

'Tis he the common people love so much.

For I myself have often heard them say,

When I've walked among them like a private man,   75
That in Lucius' banishment I was wrong,
And they have wished that he were emperor
TAMORA
Why should you fear? Is not your city strong?
SATURNINUS
Ay, but the citizens favor Lucius
And will revolt from me to strengthen him.   80
TAMORA
King, be your thoughts imperious as your name.
Is the sun dimmed if gnats do fly in it?
The eagle suffers little birds to sing
And is not bothered what they mean by it,
He knows that with the shadow of his wings   85
He can at pleasure stop their melody.
Even so may *you* Rome's giddy people.
Then cheer your spirit, for know, my emperor,
I will go enchant the old Andronicus
With words more sweet and much more dangerous   90
Than bait to fish, or honey stalks to sheep,
As the one is wounded with the bait,
The other rotted with delicious feed.
SATURINUS
But he will not call off his son for us.
TAMORA
If Tamora entreat him, then he will,   95
For I can smooth and fill his aged ears
With golden promises, that were his heart
Almost impregnable, his old ears deaf,
Yet will his ears and heart obey my tongue.
(to Aemilius)
Go you before and be our ambassador.   100

Say that the Emperor requests a parley
Of warlike Lucius, and appoint the meeting
At his father's house, the old Andronicus.

SATURNINUS

Aemilius, take the message to him
And if he demand a hostage for his safety,   105
Bid him ask what shall him satisfy.

AEMILIUS

I go at once to execute your bidding.

He exits

TAMORA

Now will I to that old Andronicus
And work him o'er with all the art I have
To pluck proud Lucius from the warlike Goths.   110
And now, sweet emperor, be blithe again,
And bury all your fears in my device.

SATURNINUS

Then go to your success, and plead with him.

They exit

ACT 5 ◆ SCENE 1

Flourish. Enter Lucius with an army of Goths,
with Drums and Soldiers

LUCIUS

Battle-tested warriors and faithful friends,
I have receivèd letters from great Rome
That pour forth the hate they bear the emperor
And how much they long for sight of us.
Therefore, great lords, be as your titles witness,   5
As kings, who will not tolerate their wrongs,
And if Rome hath done you injury,
Let him take triple satisfaction.

FIRST GOTH

Brave shoot sprung from the root of great Andronicus
Whose name was once our terror, now our joy,   10
Whose high exploits and honorable deeds
Ungrateful Rome returned with foul contempt,
Take heart in us. We'll follow where you lead
Like stinging bees in hottest summer's day
Led by their master to the flowered fields,   15
And be avenged on cursèd Tamora.

GOTHS

And as he say, so say we.

LUCIUS

I humbly thank him and I thank you all
But who comes, led by yon sturdy Goth?

Enter a Goth, leading on Aaron with his child in his arms

SECOND GOTH

Renowned Lucius, from our troops I strayed   20

85

To gaze upon a ruinous monastery,
(Wondering how it came, full three centuries
Before its time —)
And as I earnestly did fix mine eye
Upon the wasted building, suddenly   25
I heard a child cry beneath a wall.
I made unto the noise, when soon I heard
The crying babe reproached with these words:
"Peace, tawny slave, half me and half thy dame! Did
Not thy hue announce whose brat thou art,   30
Had nature lent you but thy mother's look,
Villain, thou mightst have been an emperor.
But where the bull and cow are both milk-white,
They never do beget a coal-black calf.
Peace, villain, peace!" — like so he chides the babe — 35
"For I must bear thee to a trusty Goth
Who, when he knows thou art the Empress' babe,
Will hold thee dearly for thy mother's sake."
With this, my weapon drawn, I rushed upon him,
Surprised him suddenly, and brought him here   40
To use as you think needful of the man.

LUCIUS

O worthy Goth, this is that devil in the flesh
That robbed Andronicus of his good hand;
This is the pearl that pleased your empress' eye;
And here's the base fruit of her burning lust. —   45
Say, glowering slave, whither wouldst convey
This growing image of your fiendlike face?
Why dost not speak? What, deaf? Not a word? —
A halter, soldiers! Hang him on this tree,
And by his side his fruit of bastardy.   50

AARON

Touch not the boy. He is of royal blood.

LUCIUS

Too like the sire for ever being good.

First hang the child, that he may see it kicking.

A sight to vex the father's soul withal.

Get me a ladder.   55

A ladder is brought, which Aaron is made to climb

AARON

Lucius, save the child

And bear it from me to the Empress

If you do this I'll tell to you such things

That highly may advantage you to hear.

If you will not, befall what may befall,   60

I'll speak no more but "Vengeance rot you all!"

LUCIUS

Say on, and if it please me what you speak,

The child shall live, and I will see it raised.

AARON

And if it please you? I assure you, Lucius,

'Twill scald your soul to hear what I shall speak;   65

I will unfold of murders, rapes, and massacres,

Acts of black night, abominable deeds,

Reveals of mischief, treason, villainies,

Horrible to hear, more monstrous to perform.

And this shall all be buried in my death,   70

Unless you swear to me my child shall live.

LUCIUS

Tell me your mind. I say your child shall live.

AARON

Swear that he shall, and then I will begin.

LUCIUS

Who should I swear by? You believe no god.

That granted, how can you believe an oath?   75

AARON

What if I do not? As indeed I do not.

But yet I know that you are religious

And have a thing within you called a conscience,

With twenty popish tricks and ceremonies

Which I have seen you careful to observe,   80

Therefore I trust your oath; because I know

If an idiot holds a bauble for a god

He'll keep the oath which by that god he swears.

To that I'll bind him. Therefore you shall vow

By your god, what god soe'er it be   85

That you adore and hold in reverence,

To save my boy, to nourish and bring him up

Or else be sure I will tell thee nothing.

LUCIUS

Even by my god I swear that I will.

AARON

First know that I begot him on the Empress.   90

LUCIUS

Oh, most insatiable and luxurious woman!

AARON

Tut, Lucius, this was but a pleasant prologue —

Compared to that which happened in the *second* act

'Twas her two sons that murdered Bassianus.

They cut your sister's tongue and ravished her,   95

And hacked her hands and pruned her as thou sawest.

LUCIUS

O detestable villain, call'st that pruning?

AARON

Ask them that had the trimming of her!

LUCIUS

O barbarous, beastly villains like to you!

AARON

Indeed, I was the tutor did instruct them, 100

Their loving spirit had they from their mother,

As sure as shootin' ever hit the prick;

Their bloody mind, I think they learned — of me,

As wolves learn young how to a jugular tug.

Well, let my deeds be witness of my worth. 105

The brethren invited to the fatal hole

Where the corpse of Bassianus lay;

I wrote the letter that your father found

I hid the gold of which that letter spoke,

Confederate with the queen and her two sons. 110

And what not done, that you have cause to wail,

Wherein my hand had not a hand in it — Oh.

For your father's hand I played the taxman

Collected what was due, and held myself apart

And almost cracked my ribs! So hard I laughed. 115

'Twas I peered through the crevice of a wall

When, in one hand, he held his two son's heads;

Beheld his tears and then my laughter shook

So I did cry as full and hard as he!

And when I told the empress of this sport 120

She almost fainted at my pleasing tale,

And for my tidings gave me twenty kisses.

GOTH

What, can say all of this and never blush!

AARON

Oh, but I am! Why, can you not tell?

LUCIUS

    Hast no regrets at all for these foul deeds?   125

AARON

    Regrets? That I did not do

    — a thousand more! —

    (Had I but *applied* myself) but to be fair,

    Not many came within my curse's range —

    Where I did not do something truly bad …   130

    (Or worse)

    As Kill a man, or else, to plan his death;

    Ravish a maid or plot the way to do it;

    Accuse some innocent by lying through my teeth;

    Set deadly enmity between two friends;   135

    Make poor men's cattle break their necks; Ha HA!

    Set fire to barns and haystacks to the fright

    Of those who ran to quench them with their tears.

    Oft have I digged up dead men from their graves

    And set them upright at their dear friends' door,   140

    Waiting till their grief was almost done,

    And on their skins, as on the bark of trees,

    Have with my knife in Roman letters carved

    "Let not your sorrow die, though I am dead."

    (Too much?)   145

    Oh, I have done a thousand dreadful things

    As willingly as one would kill a fly,

    And nothing do I feel of grief or sorrow

    But that I cannot do ten thousand more.

LUCIUS   150

    Bring down the devil for he must not die

    So sweet a death as present hanging.

            Aaron is brought down from the ladder

AARON

    If there be devils, would I were one,

    And live and burn in everlasting fire,

    So I might have your company in hell   155

    But to torment you with my bitter tongue.

LUCIUS

    Sirs, stop his mouth, and let him speak no more.

                   Enter Aemilius

GOTH

    My lord, there is a messenger from Rome

    Desires to be admitted to your presence

(Aemilius comes forward)

    Welcome, Aemilius. What's the news from Rome?   160

AEMILIUS

    Lord Lucius, and you princes of the Goths,

    The Roman Emperor greets you all by me;

    And, for he understands that you are armed,

    He craves a parley at your father's house,

    And bids you ask what hostages you will,   165

    And they shall be immediately delivered.

GOTH

    What says our general?

LUCIUS

    Aemilius, let the Emperor give his pledges

    Unto my father and my uncle Marcus,

    And we will come. March away.   170

                   They exit

ACT 5 ◆ SCENE 2

Enter Tamora and her two sons, disguised

TAMORA

    And so in this ridiculous disguise —

I will beguile the mad Andronicus
And say I am Revenge, sent from below
To join with him and help him with his play.
Knock at his study, where they say he keeps   5
A box of plots left over from the Greeks
Tell him Revenge is come to lend a hand
Where he has none, to work confusion on his critics.

They knock, and Titus (above) opens his study door

TITUS

Who doth molest my contemplation?
Is it your trick to make me ope the door,   10
That so my sad scribblings may fly away
And all my study be to no effect?
You are deceived, for what I mean to do,
See here, in bloody lines I have set down,
And what is written it shall be done.   15

TAMORA

Titus, I am come to talk with you.

TITUS

No, not a word. How can I grace my talk,
Wanting a hand to give it action?
You have me at a social disadvantage
Therefore go away.   20

TAMORA

If you did know me, you would talk with me.

TITUS

I am not mad. I know thee well enough.
Witness this wretched stump; I wore it down by writing;
Witness the crimson lines — I inked them with my blood —
Witness these tear troughs made by grief and care;   25
Witness the tiring day and heavy night —
Witness in my sorrow that I know thee well

As my fickle inspiration, mighty Tamora.
Is not thy coming for my other hand?

TAMORA

Know, you sad man, I am not Tamora.   30
She is your enemy, and I your friend.
I am your revenge, your longed-for climax
Sent from th'infernal kingdom down below
To finish off your stallèd tale and
Ease the gnawing vulture of thy mind   35
By working reeking vengeance on your foes.
Come from your study and join me in the light
Confer with me of murder and of death.
There's not a hollow cave or lurking place,
No vast obscurity or misty vale   40
Where bloody murder or detested rape
Can hide for fear but I will find them out,
And in their ears tell them my dreadful name
Revenge, which makes the people clap
And foul offender quake.   45

TITUS

Art thou Revenge? And art thou sent to me
To be a torment to mine enemies?

TAMORA

I am. Therefore come down and welcome me.

TITUS

Do me some service ere I come to thee.
Lo, by thy side, where Rape and Murder stands   50
Now give some demonstration th'art Revenge;
Stab them, or tear them on thy chariot wheels,
And then I'll come and be thy wagoner,
And whirl along with thee about the "Globe,"
Provide thee proper ponies, black as jet,   55

To haul the vengeful wagon swift away,
And murderers expose in guilty caves.
And when thy car is laden with their heads,
I will dismount and by thy wagon wheel
Trot like a servile footman all day long,   60
Even from Hyperion's rising in the east
Until his very downfall in the sea.
And day by day I'll do this heavy task,
(So thou destroy Rape and Murder there.)

TAMORA

These are my ministers and come with me.   65

TITUS

Are they thy ministers? What are they called?

TAMORA

Rape and Murder; as you said. For 'tis theirs
To take revenge on men that do those things.

TITUS

How like the Empress' sons they are, dead ringers.
And you the Empress! But we worldly men   70
Have miserable, mad, mistaking eyes.
O sweet Revenge, now do I come to you,
And if one arm's embracement will content,
I will wrap thee in it by and by.

He exits above

TAMORA

This agreement in him fits his lunacy.   75
Whatever I devise to feed his fantasies,
Do you uphold and maintain with your words.
For now he firmly takes me for Revenge;
And, while he's taken in by this mad thought,
I'll make him send for Lucius his son;   80
And when I at a banquet hold him safe,

I will some cunning reason there invent
To scatter and disperse the giddy Goths,
Or, at the least to turn them into foes.
See, here he comes, and I must ply my theme. 85

Enter Titus

TITUS

Long have I been forlorn, in wait for you.
Welcome, dread Revenge, to my woeful house. —
Rapine and Murder, you are welcome too.
How like the Empress and her sons you are!
Well are you fitted had you but a Moor. 90
Could not all hell afford you such a devil?
For well I know the Empress never wags
But at her tail there is a Moor;
And, would you play the Queen and fit the part
Such a devil would perfect it. 95
But welcome as you are. What's next. She speaks!

TAMORA

What wouldst thou have us do, Andronicus?

DEMETRIUS

Show me a murderer; I'll deal with him.

CHIRON

Show me a villain that hath done a rape,
And I am made to be revenged on him. 100

TAMORA

Show me a thousand that hath done thee wrong,
And I will be revenged on them all.

TITUS *(to Demetrius)*

Look round about the wicked streets of Rome,
And when you find a man that looks like you,
Good Murder, stab him; he's a murderer. 105

(to Chiron)

    Go you with him, and when you chance
    To find another that is the twin to thee,
    Good Rapist, stab him, he is a ravisher.

(to Tamora)

    Go with them; and in the Emperor's court
    There is a queen attended by a Moor.   110
    You will know her, for up and down — she's thee,
    Then do, I pray, on them some violent death.
    They have been violent to me and mine.

TAMORA

    Well have you said; so how think you of this —
    Why not, if it please you, good Andronicus,   115
    Send for Lucius, your thrice-valiant son,
    Who leads towards Rome a band of warlike Goths,
    And bid him come and banquet at your house?
    Then, when he is here, even at the solemn feast,
    Will I bring in the Empress and her sons,   120
    The Emperor himself, and all your foes,
    And for your mercy shall they stoop and kneel,
    And on them shalt you enact Catharsis by me. Revenge.
    What says Andronicus to this device?

TITUS *(calling)*

    Marcus, my brother, 'tis sad Titus calls.   125

Enter Marcus

    Go, gentle Marcus, to thy nephew Lucius.
    You shall search him out among the Goths.
    Bid him make haste to me and bring with him
    Some of the chiefest princes of the Goths.
    Bid him encamp his soldiers where they are.   130
    Tell him the Emperor and the Empress too
    Feast at my house, and he shall feast with them.

This do you for my love, and so let him
As he regards his agèd father's life.
MARCUS
This will I do, and soon return again.   135

Marcus exits

TAMORA
Now will I hence about this business
And take my ministers along with me.
TITUS
Nay, nay, let Rape and Murder stay with me,
Or else I'll call my brother back again
And cleave to no revenge but Lucius.   140
TAMORA *(aside to Chiron and Demetrius)*
What say you, boys? Will you stay here with him
Whilst I go tell my lord the Emperor
How we'll further play the joke we spoke of?
Yield to his humor, smooth and speak him fair,
But do not leave his side till I return.   145
TITUS *(aside)*
I know them all, though they suppose me mad,
And will outdo them in their own devices —
A pair of cursed hellhounds and their dam!
DEMETRIUS *(aside to Tamora)*
Madam, depart at pleasure. Leave us here.
TAMORA
Farewell, Andronicus. Revenge now goes   150
To doctor your grief and destroy your foes.
TITUS
I know you can; Sweet Revenge, farewell.

Tamora exits

CHIRON
Tell us old man, how we may serve your turn.

TITUS

Tut, I have work enough for you to do. —
Publius, come; Caius and Valentine.

Publius, Caius, and Valentine enter

PUBLIUS

What is your will? 155

TITUS

Know you these two?

PUBLIUS

The Empress' sons, I take them — Chiron, Demetrius.

TITUS

Fie, Publius, fie, what a thing to say!
The one is Murder, and Rape is the other's name;
And therefore bind them, gentle Publius. 160
Caius and Valentine, lay hands on them.
Oft have you heard me wish for such an hour,
And now I find it. Therefore bind them tight,
Oh. And gag them if they start to cry.

Titus exits

CHIRON

Villains, Unhand us. — (I mean, Forbear!) We are the 165
Empress' sons.

PUBLIUS

Ay, and so do we what we're commanded. —
Stop close their mouths; let them not speak a word.
Is he sure bound? Look that you bind them fast.

Enter Titus Andronicus with a knife, and Lavinia with a basin

TITUS

Come, come, Lavinia. See, thy foes are caught. 170
Sirs, stop their mouths. Let them not speak to me,
But hear the fearful words I say to them.
O villains, Chiron and Demetrius!

Here stands the virgin spring whom you polluted,
This goodly summer blighted by your winter.   175
You killed her husband, and for that vile fault
Two of her brothers were condemned to death,
My hand cut off, my misery mocked
Her hands ripped, her tongue torn, and that more dear
Than hands or tongue, her tender innocence,   180
Inhuman traitors, you plundered and destroyed.
What could you say if I should let you speak?
You foreswore grace and cannot beg for it.
But hark, wretches, how I mean to martyr you.
This one hand yet is left to cut your throats   185
While Lavinia between her stumps will hold
The basin to receive your guilty blood.
You know your mother means to feast with me,
And calls herself Revenge and thinks me mad?
She might be right. Now list what I will do.   190
Hark, villains, I will grind your bones to dust,
And with your blood and it, I'll make a paste,
And of the paste a coffin I will rear
And make two pasties of your shameful heads,
And bid that strumpet, your unhallowed dam,   195
Like to the earth swallow her own increase.
This is the feast that I have bid her to,
And this banquet shall the Gorgon gorge on!
Far worse than Philomel you used my daughter,
And as Procne took her vengeance so will I —   200
And so prepare your throats. — Lavinia, come,
Receive the blood. (You'll need another bowl)
(he cuts their throats)
Now by a family recipe — when dead —
I will go grind their bones to powder small,

99

And with this hateful liquor mix it well, 205
And in that paste shall bake their vile heads.
Chop Chop! Lend me your hands! I mean on deck!
To make this banquet better than the Centaurs' feast!
So. Bring them in, and I will play the cook
And see that dinner's ready when their mother comes. 210

They exit carrying the dead bodies

ACT 5 ◆ SCENE 3

Enter Lucius, Marcus and the Goths, with Aaron, Guards,
and an Attendant carrying the baby

LUCIUS

Uncle Marcus, if it is my father's will
That I repair to Rome I am content.

FIRST GOTH

And ours with yours, befall what fortune will.

LUCIUS

Good Uncle, take you this barbarous Moor,
This ravenous tiger, this accursed devil. 5
Give him neither food nor drink. Chain him
Till he be brought unto the Empress' face
For witness of her foul proceedings
And see our friends lie ready in ambush.
I fear the Emperor means no good to us. 10

AARON

Some devil whisper curses in my ear
And prompt me that my tongue may spit
The malicious venom of my swelling heart.

LUCIUS

Away inhuman dog, unhallowed slave!
Sirs, help our uncle to convey him in. 15

Trumpets sound, showing the Emperor is at hand,

Guards and Aaron exit.

Enter Emperor Saturninus and Empress Tamora with Aemilius,
Tribunes, Attendants, and others.

SATURNINUS

What, has the firmament more suns than one?

LUCIUS

What avails it you to call yourself a sun?

MARCUS

Emperor, and nephew, 'tis time to "parle."

These quarrels must be quietly debated.

The feast is ready which the careful Titus   20

Hath ordained to an honorable end.

For peace, for love, for league and good to Rome.

Please you therefore draw near and take your places.

SATURNINUS

Marcus, we will.

Trumpets sounds

Enter Titus like a cook, placing the dishes, with young Lucius and
others, and Lavinia with a veil over her face

TITUS

Welcome, my lords, welcome, dread queen   25

Welcome you warlike Goths, welcome Lucius

And welcome all. Although simple be the cheer,

'Twill fill your stomachs. Please you eat of it,

And till the Emperor and his wife be fed

As the saying goes — *Familius tenus bakus* —   30

Family Hold Back!

(And you too, Warlike Goths, I most advise.)

Tamora and Saturninus eat

SATURNINUS

Why are you so attired, Andronicus?

TITUS

Why, to prepare this feast with my own hand.
A family recipe, for honored guests.   35
I thought it might be better servèd cold —
How think you?

TAMORA

Nay, I cannot get enough, Good Andronicus.

TITUS

Oh, you shall — (If you only knew my heart)
My Lord the Emperor, riddle me this: 40
I've heard the story of a man — Virginius
Did slay his daughter with his own right hand
Because she had been Deflowered. Stained. Raped.
Did he do right? In your opinion?

SATURNINUS

Hmm. Yes, I believe he did, Andronicus.   45

TITUS

Your reason, mighty lord?

SATURNINUS

Because the girl should not survive her shame.
And by her presence still remind his sorrows.

TITUS

A reason mighty strong, and practical;
A pattern historical and living instruction both   50
For me, most wretched, to perform the like.
Die, die, Lavinia, and thy shame with thee,
And with thy shame thy father's sorrow die.

He kills Lavinia

SATURNINUS

What have you done, unnatural and unkind!?

TITUS

Freed her for whom my tears have made me blind.   55

I am as Virginius was,

And have a thousand times more cause than he

To do this outrage, and it now 'tis done.

SATURNINUS

What, was she ravished? Tell who did the deed.

TITUS

You've scarce touched your plate. Will it please you eat?   60

TAMORA

Why have you slain your only daughter thus?

TITUS

Not I, but Chiron and Demetrius.

They ravished her and hacked away her tongue,

And they, 'twas they, that slayed her —

SATURNINUS

Go at once fetch them here to us!   65

TITUS

Oh, but they are here — both baked in a pie

Whereof their mother daintily has fed,

Eating the flesh that she herself has bred.

Tis true, 'tis true, as sure as my knife's point.

He stabs the Empress

SATURNINUS

Die, frantic wretch, for this accursed deed.   70

He kills Titus

LUCIUS

Shall I stand by and see my father bleed?

(he kills Saturninus)

There's blow for blow, death for deadly deed.

Great tumult. Lucius, Marcus, and others go to upper stage.

MARCUS

You broken citizens, you sons of Rome,

By these uproars scattered as a flight of fowl

Tossed by winds and high tempestuous gusts, 75
O, let us teach ourselves to gather back
This scattered corn into one mutual sheaf,
To Knit these broken limbs into one body,
Lest Rome do final execution on herself.
Here's Rome's young captain. Let him tell the tale, 80
While I stand by and weep to hear him speak.

LUCIUS

Then, gracious listeners, be it known to you
That Chiron and the damned Demetrius
Were they that murdered our emperor's brother,
And they it were that ruined our sister. 85
For their savagery our brothers lost their heads
Our father's tears mocked, he basely tricked
To give his hand, true hand that fought for Rome
And sent her enemies unto the grave;
And last myself, unkindly banishèd, 90
The gates barred on me, I cast weeping out
To beg relief among Rome's enemies
Who drowned their enmity in my true tears
And oped their arms to take me as their friend.
I am the turned-forth, be it known to you, 95
That have preserved Rome's welfare in my blood
And from her bosom took the enemy's point,
And turned it to my own-adventured body.
Alas you see these proofs of what I tell
My scars can witness, dumb although they are, 100
That my report is just and true.

MARCUS

Behold the child.
Of this was Tamora delivered,
The issue of a sacrilegious Moor,

Chief architect and plotter of these woes.   105
The villain is alive in Titus' house,
And as he to you will witness, this is true.
Now have you heard the truth. What say you, Romans?
Have we wrongly done?

ROMANS

Lucius, all hail, Rome's royal emperor!   110

AEMILIUS

The common voice do cry it shall be so,

MARCUS *(to attendants)*

Go, go into old Titus' sorrowful house,
And hither haul the Moorish infidel
To judgment and a direful slaught'ring death
As punishment for his most wicked life.   115

Attendants exit

Lucius and Marcus come down from the upper stage

ROMANS

Lucius, all hail, Rome's gracious governor!

LUCIUS

Thanks, gentle Romans. May I govern so
To heal Rome's harms and wipe away her woe!
But, gentle people, give me leave awhile,
For nature puts me to a heavy task.   120
Stand you all aloof, but, uncle draw you near
To shed our mourning tears upon his earth.

(he kisses Titus)

O, take this warm kiss on thy pale cold cheek.
These sorrowful drops upon thy bloodstained face,
The last true duties of thy last-remaining son   125

MARCUS *(he kisses Titus)*

O, were the sum of these that I should pay
Countless and infinite, yet would I pay them.

LUCIUS *(to Young Lucius)*

    Come hither boy. Come, come and learn of us

    How tears can melt thee. Thy grandsire loved thee well.

MARCUS

    O, now, sweet boy, give him a last kiss.   130

    Bid him farewell; commit him to the grave.

    Do him that kindness, and take leave of him.

YOUNG LUCIUS

    O grandsire, grandsire, ev'n with all my heart

    I had so hoped to go to war with you!

(he kisses Titus)

    O Lord, I cannot speak to him for weeping.   135

    My tears will choke me if I further speak.

               Enter Aaron with guards

A ROMAN

    You sad Andronici, bury your woes.

    Give sentence on the abominable wretch

    That hath been father of these harsh events

LUCIUS

    Set him breast-deep in the earth and starve him.   140

    There let him stand and rave and cry for food.

    If anyone relieves or pities him,

    For the offense they die. See it done.

    Some stay to see him fastened in the ground.

AARON

    Think you my rage is mute, my fury dumb?   145

    Or I some baby, that with whimp'ring prayer

    Will now repent the evils I have done.

    Why, ten thousand worse than ever yet I did

    Would I perform (if I might have my dream)

    If one good deed in all my life I did —   150

    For this, God, I am most heartily sorry.

Aaron is led off by Guards

LUCIUS

Some loving friends bear the Emperor hence
And give him burial in his father's grave.
My father and Lavinia shall presently
Be closèd in our ancestral tomb.   155
As for that ravenous tiger, Tamora —
No funeral rite, nor man in black;
No mournful bell shall ring her burial —
Tamora's voice may join his
But cast her forth unto the wilderness   160
And let those beasts and birds that will, prey.

They exit, carrying off the dead bodies

END